Tiny Hinsdale
of the Silvery San Juan

by
Carolyn and Clarence Wright

WESTERN REFLECTIONS PUBLISHING COMPANY®
Lake City, Colorado

An authorized reprint published by
Western Reflections Publishing Company
P.O. Box 1149
951 N. Highway 149
Lake City, CO 81235

www.westernreflectionspublishing.com

© 2012 Marilyn Wright Plise, Claire Wright Martinez, and Nancy Wright Norland
All rights reserved

Cover art and design by Angela Hollingsworth
APH creative design, Lake City, CO
Cover photograph: The Town of Lake City, circa 1882, looking south.

Printed in the United States of America

ISBN 978-1-937851-08-8

INTRODUCTION

In 1964, after "intense work, research and devotion to task," Clarence and Carolyn Wright proudly published the first edition of *Tiny Hinsdale of The Silvery San Juan* and lovingly dedicated it to their four grandchildren: Nancy Louise (Wright) Norland, Claire Francis (Wright) Martinez, Marilyn Lucille (Wright) Plise and Walter Clarence Wright (killed in action in Vietnam, October 3rd, 1967 –USAF).

The Wrights' dedication to this work is recalled by their living grandchildren through vivid memories and visions of their Grandma working feverishly for months and months typing on her little Smith-Corona typewriter and their Grandpa, who was almost totally blind, supervising every paragraph. It was extremely important to them to document the history and true happenings in and around Hinsdale County.

The Wright Family and their descendants are very proud of their family history in Hinsdale County and the legacy left them by their great grandparents, grandparents and parents. As *Tiny Hinsdale of The Silvery San Juan*, when originally published, was lovingly dedicated to the authors' grandchildren, their granddaughters are now in the same loving spirit pleased and proud to grant permission for this history of Hinsdale County, Colorado to be republished and serve as a memorial to their grandparents' devoted efforts.

Carolyn Wright passed away suddenly August 12, 1970 in Gunnison, Colorado at the age of 80. Clarence E. Wright graced the lives of his son, granddaughters, and the lives of his great grandchildren until August 29, 1980, when he passed away peacefully in his 94th year at the home of his only son, William C. Wright in Montrose, Colorado.

At the time of this republication, they are survived by three granddaughters, who feel blessed to have had the love, encouragement and guidance of their grandparents.

Clarence and Carolyn are also survived by four-great grandsons - Donald Norland, Dennis Norland, William Walter Plise, and Robert Plise; three great granddaughters - Lara Martinez, Linda (Martinez) Mauney, and Carrie (Plise) Delatorre; and eight great-great grandchildren.

The Wright granddaughters "make like mountain goats" and visit "The View of the Park" (aka Park View) back in 1995. Left to right - Marilyn Wright Plise, Claire Wright Martinez and Nancy Wright Norland in front of their mine located on Edith Mountain. (See page 159 – photograph with similar view - "Looking north from Edith Mountain toward Red Cloud Peak" - taken by Clarence Wright in the early 1900s).

ABOUT THE AUTHORS

Clarence Wright was born in Lake City in 1886. He attended the Lake City schools through the tenth grade, when his parents moved to San Diego, California, where he graduated from high school. After his father's death, the family returned to Colorado and settled in Boulder, where his elder brother was a senior at the state university and where he entered preparatory school. He returned to Lake City each summer to keep up the assessment on the family mines. In the spring of 1908 he came back to stay. He was married to Carolyn Hunt February 25, 1911. In 1914 he was appointed postmaster at Lake City, a position he held until 1935. During his 21 years as postmaster he received reappointment certificates signed by President Harding in 1921, President Coolidge in 1925 and President Hoover in 1931. He and Mrs. Wright later owned and operated a café. In 1935 he was appointed Hinsdale County Welfare Director and received many awards from the Welfare Department during his tenure. While he was postmaster he was awarded a silver loving cup from Hinsdale County.

Carolyn Hunt Wright was born in Grand Junction August 8, 1890. She moved with her parents to Lake City at the age of seven. A graduate of the Lake City high school, she later attended normal school at Greeley. After teaching several years, she returned to school at Western State College. She taught school both in Hinsdale and Gunnison Counties, and served as county superintendent of schools for sixteen years, her last term being from 1948 through 1958. She began working as a newspaper reporter in 1933, writing for the *Gunnison News Champion*, *Grand Junction Sentinel* and the *Lake City Tribune*, of which she was the associate editor. She also did spot news for the *Denver Post*. She had a number of songs and poems published. She published a short history of Hinsdale County in 1960. She served as Cancer Captain and was chairman of the T.B. Society. She received an award for war work during the First World War, was a member of the Ladies Aid, and was a member of the Federated Women's Club, for which she was State Chairman of Conservation for four years.

TINY HINSDALE
OF
THE SILVERY SAN JUAN

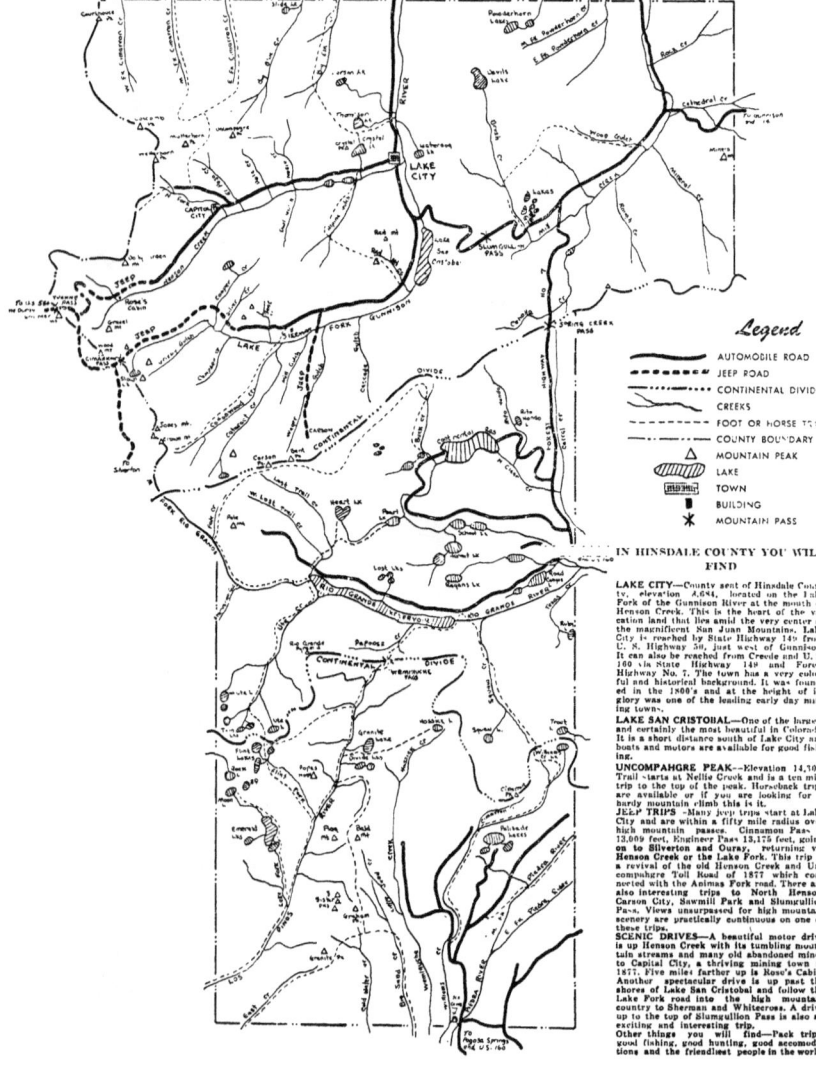

IN HINSDALE COUNTY YOU WILL FIND

LAKE CITY—County seat of Hinsdale County, elevation 8,641, located on the Lake Fork of the Gunnison River at the mouth of Henson Creek. This is the heart of the vacation land that lies amid the very center of the magnificent San Juan Mountains. Lake City is reached by State Highway 149 from U. S. Highway 50, just west of Gunnison. It can also be reached from Creede and U. S. 160 via State Highway 149 and Forest Highway No. 7. The town has a very colorful and historical background. It was founded in the 1800's and at the height of its glory was one of the leading early day mining towns.

LAKE SAN CRISTOBAL—One of the largest and certainly the most beautiful in Colorado. It is a short distance south of Lake City and boats and motors are available for good fishing.

UNCOMPAHGRE PEAK—Elevation 14,306. Trail starts at Nellie Creek and is a ten mile trip to the top of the peak. Horseback trips are available or if you are looking for a hardy mountain climb this is it.

JEEP TRIPS—Many jeep trips start at Lake City and are within a fifty mile radius over high mountain passes. Cinnamon Pass is 13,000 feet, Engineer Pass 13,175 feet, going on to Silverton and Ouray, returning via Henson Creek or the Lake Fork. This trip is a revival of the old Henson Creek and Uncompahgre Toll Road of 1877 which connected with the Animas Fork road. There are also interesting trips to North Henson, Carson City, Sawmill Park and Slumgullion Pass. Views unsurpassed for high mountain scenery are practically continuous on one of these trips.

SCENIC DRIVES—A beautiful motor drive is up Henson Creek with its tumbling mountain streams and many old abandoned mines to Capital City, a thriving mining town in 1877. Five miles farther up is Rose's Cabin. Another spectacular drive is up past the shores of Lake San Cristobal and follow the Lake Fork road into the high mountain country to Sherman and Whitecross. A drive up to the top of Slumgullion Pass is also an exciting and interesting trip.

Other things you will find—Pack trips, good fishing, good hunting, good accommodations and the friendliest people in the world.

TINY HINSDALE

of

The Silvery San Juan

Carolyn and Clarence Wright

1964 © by Carolyn and Clarence Wright

To our Grandchildren

This Book is Lovingly Dedicated.

TABLE OF CONTENTS

Introduction	10
Origins	11
Revolt of the 1940's	17
Early Mining	22
Strike of the Ute-Ulay and Hidden Treasure	27
Newspapers	29
Post Offices	32
War Saving and Thrift Stamps	37
Roads	38
Areas and Mines around Lake City	45
The Railroad	50
Snowslides	58
Libraries	61
Hinsdale County Schools	62
The First Presbyterian Church of Lake City and Other Churches	69
Fires and Early Buildings	75
Firefighting	79
Electricity	81
Telephone	83
Water Works Bonds	85
Early-day Entertainment and Recreation	87
Lodges and the Pitkin Guard	103
Hotels	106
Lakes and Fishing	112
Lake San Cristobal	116
Lake San Cristobal—poem	121
Crime	123
Packer the Cannibal	128
Sheriff Campbell Shot Dead	133
The Duel	138
Hell's Acres	140
When Congressman Bell Sat on a Stump	142
W. H. Brewster, Hermit	144
Tales of Pike Snowden	146
Lena Wright	149
Harry E. Wright	155
Other Pioneers	160
Quotes from Old Newspapers	187
About the Authors	192
Acknowledgments	193
Bibliography	195

TABLE OF ILLUSTRATIONS

First cabin in Lake City	10
Lake City looking north	13
Lake City in winter	13
Lake City looking south	15
Early-day picture of Lake City, looking west	15
Lake City looking north	16
On top of Uncompaghre, Mrs. W. P. Hunt	18
On top of Uncompaghre, one can look straight down	18
Crystal Peak and lake	21
Uncompaghre Peak	21
Station Eleven	21
Balanced Rock	23
North Clear Creek Falls	23
Pack train of Jumbo Peak	26
Ute and Ulay and tramway	28
Hidden Treasure mill, office, bunkhouse	31
First Lake City post office	33
Present Lake City post office	33
First post office at Capitol City	33
Post office at White Cross	33
Last post office at Capitol City	33
La Belle Tunnel at White Cross	37
Early-day horseback riding	44
Lake City train on high bridge	49
First engine of D&RG off track	52
Engine over the grade	55
Kitchen showing under story carried away by slide	57
Recovering bodies of Cutting and Johnson	59
Holes from which two bodies were recovered	59
Hole from which body of Cutting was recovered	60
Rescuers standing in hole	60
Carrying body of Johnson	60
Bodies packed for sled trip	60
Lake City schoolhouse built in 1880	64
Schoolhouse as it looked in 1949	64
Schoolhouse after it was remodeled	66
Capitol City schoolhouse built in 1883	66
Clay modeling	68
Two view of the Presbyterian Church	70
Episcopal Church	70
Baptist Church with Sunday School, 1925	73
Catholic Church	78
Fire that destroyed Richard's Barn	78

The first Hough Volunteer Fire Company	78
A closer view of Baptist Church	80
Another view of the Empire Chief snowslide	82
Carolyn and Clarence Wright	84
Fourth of July celebration, 1897	86
Close-up of drilling contest	89
Pioneer Jubilee Club Room—before and after	89
C. E. Wright, pitcher of the Lake City Blues	98
The Green Basketball Team	98
Old timers' party	100
Pupils of Lake City school celebrating	100
Pioneers gathered at Baker ranch	102
First automobile in Lake City	105
Parlor of Old Pueblo House	108
Occidental Hotel	108
Hotel at Rose's Cabin	111
First cabin at Rose's Cabin	111
Sherman Hotel	111
A day's catch at Water Dog Lake, 1929	115
Lake San Cristobal	115
Boats on Lake San Cristobal about 1894	115
Slumgullion "break off"	120
Packing ties at VC Bar Ranch	122
Pet elk	122
Packer Club card	127
Site of Packer massacre	127
Alfred Packer	132
Hinsdale County Court Room	132
The old stage stop (two views)	137
Walter Wright playing handmade banjo	143
Pike Snowden	145
Grandma Wright at 101 years	150
Grandma Wright and her family	150
The White Cross on White Cross Mountain	154
Edith Mountain	158
Looking north from Edith Mountain	159
Crookes Falls	159
J. A. Woods' mule team	159
Rex Schafer	165
Miners' and Merchants' Bank	165
Old planing mill	165
Old Harry Youmans' Ranch	166
Harry Youmans and C. P. Foster	166
Toll gate	166
The Lee mansion	172
Willis Williams on Jim	172
Lake City looking toward T Mountain	172
Mrs. H. E. Wright and Mrs. Moritz Stockder	186

INTRODUCTION

Because so many authors with a flair for historical sketches have gone from place to place gathering material, which many of them no doubt thought authentic, and have published articles about different parts of Colorado which are not true, we have decided to write about the true happenings in and about this area, where we, as descendants of the real pioneers, grew up.

Our parents came to Lake City in covered wagons, the Wrights in the 70's and the Hunts in the 80's, as will be described in the book. We not only remember the stories they told us, but have their diaries which were written on the way here and after they arrived. We also have the scrapbooks made by both our mothers, containing clippings from the papers as far back as 1876, as well as many of the papers dating from that time.

The first cabin in Lake City, built by Enos Hotchkiss.

ORIGINS

Hinsdale County, nicknamed "Tiny Hinsdale," because it is the smallest county in population in the United States, is situated in the Eastern part of the great San Juan, and is the most promising part of this district. It was named "Hinsdale" in honor of George A. Hinsdale, an attorney from Pueblo, who served as lieutenant governor in 1865.

This county was organized from parts of Conejos, Costilla and Lake Counties in 1874. The eastern boundary was changed in 1893 when Mineral County was organized during the boom days of Creede, and segregated all that portion east of the Continental Divide which makes a huge loop toward the San Juan Mountains. It was prospected as early as 1869.

Hinsdale County is seventy miles long with an average width of thirty miles. The first county seat was San Juan City, which is now known as Officers Ranch. However, more people settled in Lake City than in San Juan City, and early in the fall, according to the *San Juan Crescent*, a special election was held and the voters decided to move the county seat to Lake City.

The first county election was held in September, 1874, and the following officers were elected: J. M. Sweeney, Sheriff; W. H. Green. County Clerk and Recorder; B. L. Jones, Treasurer; W. R. Kennedy, County Attorney; A. R. Thompson, Probate Judge; H. H. Wilcox, County Assessor; H. Franklin, J. J. Holbrook, and Enos Hotchkiss, County Commissioners.

The first cabin built in Lake City was that of Enos Hotchkiss in 1874. The Bartholfs, B. A. Sherman, the Lee brothers, Finley Sparling, Brockett and others followed and the foundation of the town was laid.

The town company was then organized and the following officers elected: President, Henry Finley; Secretary, F. Newton Bogue; Treasurer, W. T. Ring. Those, with Otto Mears, Isaac Gotthelff, E. T. Hotchkiss, and H. M. Woods constituted the first board of trustees. The townsite was entered in the U. S. Land Office at Del Norte in October, 1875.

When the spring of 1875 opened the town comprised thirteen log cabins.

At the spring election April 3, 1875, Henry Finley, J. H. Hines, D. M. Watson, C. P. Foster, and Isaac Waldron were elected trustees of the town; Frank Curtis, Clerk; Oscar Downtain, Constable; and J. W. Dine, street supervisor.

The first wedding was that of D. S. Hughes and Kitty Eastman, May 14, 1875. The first sawmill was erected in May by Finley and Church.

The Presbyterian Society was organized June 18, 1875, by Reverend Alex Darley, being the first religious organization here. More will be told about Mr. Darley in the chapter on churches.

The first issue of the *Silver World* was published June 19, 1875. More about newspapers will be given later.

The first child born in the town was on July 8, 1875 to Mr. and Mrs. S. W. Hoyt. The event was chronicled in the *Silver World* as a "red letter day."

The first coach of Barlow and Sanderson's stage line arrived from Saguache July 11, 1875. From then on the stages made regular tri-weekly trips between Lake City and Saguache, carrying the mail.

The Lake City and Antelope park toll road was completed November 22, 1875. The meeting at which the company was organized was held at Del Norte June 23, 1875. The board of directors chosen at the meeting were: J. H. Shaw, Alva Adams, Herman Schiffer, Henry Finley, E. J. Shaw, and Charles Newman, secretary, E. J. Shaw, treasurer.

By November 1, 1875, the town contained sixty-seven finished buildings and about four hundred inhabitants. Rapid strides in growth and development were made during 1876. Among the principal events were the completion of the Brooke's concentration works July 4th, Van Gisson's lixiviation works in December, the sale of the Ute and Ulay Mine for the sum of $135,000, and the sale of eleven-twelfths of the Ocean Mine. These events attracted additional attention at this point and led to considerable immigration during the year. On the first of November, 1876, the population of the town was estimated at 1,000 and contained two assayers, two banks, three bakeries, three barber shops, two billiard halls, five blacksmith shops, three boot and shoe stores, two brickyards, two breweries, two cigar factories, one clothing house, five corrals and feed stables, two drug stores, one furniture house, fourteen stores dealing in general merchandise, four hardware stores, four hotels, two jewelry stores, four Chinese laundries, fifteen lawyers, four meat markets, one newspaper—the *Silver World*—three newsdealers, three painters, one planing mill, six restaurants—two open all night—seven saloons, four sawmills, one shingle mill, nine surveyors.

Lake City, looking north.

Lake City in winter.

By the first of February, 1877, building was recommenced and by March first a large number of business houses and residences were under construction.

Property advanced rapidly in value and lots which formerly sold for $250 to $300 now sold for $500 to $600. So great was the demand for lumber that the mills could not supply the demand, and the planing mill, although running day and night, could not turn out enough dressed lumber as was needed. Camps of tents and cabins housed all kinds of people during that early rush period—Americans, English, Germans, Chinese, Japanese, Irish, Italian, and Negro. The population in 1877 reached 2000 and by 1879 reached 4000.

The increase in population was not only rapid but lasting and the class of people immigrating were far superior to those who usually rush to a boom town. The coaches coming in were so loaded that by April 10 the line was forced to put on daily service. During April, May, and June the roads leading into town were lined with newcomers—pedestrians, with loads on their backs, or on burros and jacks, men on horseback and in wagons—a constant stream pouring into the San Juan through Lake City, the metropolis.

Many who came were, of course, disappointed. They came, not knowing the hardships of mining, and those not having a trade were unable to direct their energies to other channels. The exodus of this class was about as rapid as their incoming. However, business men, mechanics, men of capital, came in great numbers and stayed, and today Lake City can boast of the best class of citizens.

It is impossible to name all the men who came in the early years, but among those who came from 1874 to 1880 were Tim Clawson, Charles Schafer, J. M. Michaels, Robert Kissack, E. T. and M. Hotchkiss, Peter Robinson, Robert Wagner, D. C. Baker, Herman Mayer, J. K. Mullen, L. B. Hunter, E. C. Wager, James Sloan, E. M. Slough, Andrew McLaughlin, Sr., J. M. Allen, E. L. Sleeper, J. J. and J. W. Abbott, C. D. Peck, Leonard Lowe, Charles Bent, J. E. Whinnery, Thomas and Jesse Beam, Joe Donnel, C. P. Foster, H. E. Wright, John Lowe and sisters Lena Lowe and Emma McDowell, W. I. Edgerton, John S. Hough, William Patterson, George Mott, Thomas Kirker, James Sheridan, W. G. Luckett, James and Sam Watson, Sherman Williams, D. T. McLeod, Richard James, Leon LeFevre, R. E. Penniston, Press Hix, W. P. and J. A. Hunt, W. L. Davy, W. F. Green, Charles Fuller, John Naurer and sister Amelia, Henry Maurer, John Crooke, James Steinbeck, Moritz Stocter, F. M. Mendenhall, Thomas Griffiths, John C. Bell and others. Jim Haribson, J. K. Mullen and George Boughton had made a camp near Lake City as

Lake City, looking south.

Early-day picture of Lake City, looking west.

early as 1869. All these mentioned helped in some way to make the history of Hinsdale County. Many will be mentioned later.

Hinsdale County has five of the fifty-four peaks in Colorado over 14,000 ft. high. They are: Uncompahgre, 14,301; Red Cloud, 14,050; Handies, 14,049; Sunshine, 14,018; and Wetterhorn, 14,017. Other peaks more than 13,000 ft. are: Del Norte, White Cross, Wood Mountain, Carson Peak, Gravel Mountain, Wild Horse, Stray Horse, Cox Comb, Matterhorn, Crystal Peak, Sunshine Peak, Red Mountain, Grassy, and Tumble.

Hinsdale County has a steamship named in its honor. It is the S. S. Hinsdale, Fourth Troop Transport constructed at Wilmington, California and launched July 15, 1944. A former Lake City resident, Earl Cole, was working at the shipyard at the time of the launching.

Lake City, looking north.

REVOLT OF 1940's

In the early 40's there came to Lake City investors from Texas, Arizona, New Mexico and Oklahoma. They had all vacationed here earlier and saw the possibilities of making this area a bigger and better place for tourists. Someone spread the word that the Texans were not liked by the "natives," as the residents were called. Nothing was further from the truth, but it created a feeling against the natives by all the newcomers.

As more outsiders came in and became interested in investing in Lake City, as a good place to make money, they began to get together and think of ways to get rid of the so-called "natives" who did not agree with them.

A new Chamber of Commerce was organized, and although some of the residents were asked to join, they were not consulted in any way and the officers were all chosen from the new residents.

These new investors made plans to get rid of the county officers and replace them with their own men so that they could run the county to suit themselves. The first move in this direction was a complaint to the District Attorney about the County Commissioners who, they claimed, had been negligent in that the county barn where the county machinery was housed had burned and the commissioners had carried no insurance. They were also accused of other misdemeanors. These commissioners, Joel Swank, Clarence Howard and H. T. Hoffman, resigned rather than fight although they were absolved from any blame. In spite of the fact that the republicans and democrats met in joint session to recommend men to be appointed by the governor to fill the vacancies until the next election, the governor, who had certainly been misinformed, appointed men recommended by the new faction.

The main object of the new faction in getting control of the county, was to build better roads and more fish lakes to attract the tourists. To give credit where credit is due, better roads, which were certainly needed, were built, and we all benefited from them.

On top of Uncompaghre. Mrs. W. P. Hunt—seated between the two piles of rocks—was the oldest woman ever to climb the peak.

On top of Uncompaghre. From where this picture was taken one can look straight down several thousand feet.

Not being educationally minded, the new board made a different division of the Forest money, giving only 5% to schools and 95% to roads. So many kicked about this that they later gave schools a greater percentage.

Had not the men at the head of these plans become so greedy, and so obsessed with the idea of getting rid of the people who had worked all their lives to hold on to and improve what their parents had founded, they could have done a lot of good, made a lot of money, and still have had the good will of the so-called "natives."

The fact that the new commissioners did get us better roads and other improvements led the old-time residents to vote for them at the next election in November, an act which they were soon to regret, for then they really began to show their power. Their next move was to get control of the city government. Mr. Edwards had been elected to the City Council, and started complaints about the light plant owned and operated by George Fesser, and sought to have the light plant condemned to force Fesser to sell his franchise.

It began to be rumored that more of the old timers were to go and gradually most of those who had gone along with Edwards turned against him, and a petition was circulated against him to remove him from the office of County Commissioner. When he learned of this he resigned. However, not wanting to give up, he tried again for the nomination at the next election, but was defeated. Still sticking to his guns, he then tried to back one of his followers for the office, and again he failed. The "natives" had had enough, and elected a native, Frank M. Mendenhall, who is at present chairman of the Board of County Commissioners.

The City fight went on. Friends of George Fesser, who had operated the light plant since 1947, objected to his being literally kicked out. Rather than be a party to such action, the Mayor, Frank Mendenhall, and two councilmen, Joel F. Swank and William C. Wright, resigned. They were immediately replaced by three others favoring REA. Edwards resigned as councilman and was elected Mayor by the remaining councilmen. They, with the newly appointed officer, voted to revoke Fesser's franchise and seek another power source. Frank Mendenhall is quoted as saying that he resigned because he didn't like the method used in condemning the power plant. He said the people should have been consulted before the council acted, and that he wanted no part of it. The councilmen who resigned felt the same way. At a special meeting the new council voted that the members be authorized to carry weapons. Edwards said that the town marshall's post had been discontinued for economy reasons and therefore it was necessary to place law enforcement authority with the Council. Glenn Hunt, County Sheriff, said that he had seen the minutes and that they specified that the "move was for self protection." Hunt was at odds with Edwards, who had caused his pay to be cut from $55 to $10 a month. It was definitely a squeeze move to get Hunt out of office. Hunt, in turn, deputized a group favoring Fesser and the band marched on city hall and the council meeting all armed. The majority of the residents of the town described the move on the Council as "high handed," and taken without the consent and knowledge of the local people.

Copy of the petition against George Edwards:

State of Colorado
County of Hinsdale
Petition of recall

Subject: In the matter of the Recall Petition of George Edwards, a county commissioner of Hinsdale County.
To the County Clerk of Hinsdale County, Colorado.
Take Notice:
Come the undersigned petitioners and demand an election for a successor to the office of County Commissioner District_____of Hinsdale County, Colorado, and demand an election by the qualified electors of Hinsdale County to recall the aforesaid George H. Edwards from the office of County Commissioners, of Hinsdale County District____Hinsdale County, Colorado, and in support of their petition and as the ground or grounds for this petition states as follows:
The said George H. Edwards did misuse County funds, equipment and personnel of Hinsdale County in the following:
1. Authorized the use of County funds appropriated by the Board of County Commissioners for road and bridge purposes only, for the purpose of building fish ponds and camp grounds.
2. Used County equipment to grade and gravel his own property and to haul gravel to said real property.
3. Used County employees for his own personal use.
As County Commissioner, the said George H. Edwards hired personnel from the Police Department of the City of Gunnison, Colorado to conduct an independent investigation into an alleged criminal act of vandalism against the property of said George H. Edwards, and did sign a Hinsdale County voucher authorizing payment for said investigation.
George H. Edwards individually exercised powers and functions that can only be lawfully exercised by the Board of County Commissioners of the County of Hinsdale acting in concert.

Crystal Peak and lake.

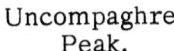

Uncompaghre Peak.

Station Eleven. McGraw photo.

EARLY MINING

The beginning of any mining camp was the early-day prospectors, who usually came in pairs. Sometimes there was a lone man and his burro, but the men would camp somewhere near each other and exchange work in the mine and in the building of their houses or cabins. The patient donkey, or sometimes a mother burro with a tiny colt, and again a sturdy jack, would pack the prospector's camp equipment, consisting of blankets, pick, shovel, and tools. The cooking equipment, a coffee pot, dutch oven, water pail and dishpan, which was used for both washing and dishes, a bake pan, hand-ax and saw, were also necessary. Food varied as to how far they were from a store where supplies could be purchased. Usually they would have coffee in the bean, which would have to be ground, salt, sugar, baking powder or cream of tartar, bacon, the grease from which was saved for the fat or lard with which to cook, dried fruits—apples, pears or peaches, beans, flour or corn meal, etc. The fresh meats were found at most of the camp sites and there were fish in the streams. Then, of course, there was the trusty gun or guns, muzzle-loaders with shot loads of various sizes and the black powder that had to be kept dry or it would be useless. One had to have the usual supply of his favorite tobacco, which, when chewed, was saved, dried and then used to smoke in the pipe. The real early pioneer did not have at his command medicines that he carried with him, but relied on nature. If the need of medicines occurred, he looked for them in the vicinity of his camp. Herbs of various kinds that could be brewed were used, or if it were a cut or sore, the best medicine he would look for would be a Balsam or Spruce tree. If there was no pitch or sap running from the bark, then a cut or two would be made with the ax to get the fresh pitch to put on the cut or open wound. Later, when there were drugstores near, a small bottle of carbolic acid would be a part of the medicine kit. A few drops of the acid, mixed with pitch from the trees and melted mutton tallow or deer fat, would make a salve that would heal any cut on man or beast.

Balanced Rock in Sparlin Gulch. Photo by William Wright.

North Clear Creek Falls. Photo by William Wright

At camp the saddles would be removed from the burros and the camp was made. The only shelter available was the trees where a wickiup was made. Bed was spread on the ground under the trees and a campfire built for cooking. The burros were turned loose. The first thing they would do was to find a good place with loose dirt to roll in, then they were ready for the grass and water. When turned loose, they never wandered far from the camp and the next morning they would come to the camp at the call of the prospector who never mistreated his best friends, the donkeys. They were very faithful if kindly treated.

Two men could put up a log cabin in a very short time. The place to build the cabin was selected, the logs cut and peeled and then the logs were notched so that the next set above would fit down in the last one. One of the main considerations for the site of a cabin was water. The early cabins did not have windows and only had one door. The floor was made of dirt and a fireplace was used for heating and cooking. When it came to the roof, a ridge pole was laid. From the ridge to the sidelogs small logs about four inches in diameter were placed side by side. These logs were laid very close together; then a foot of dirt was shoveled on the roof. After that, all that was needed in the future was to shovel more dirt on the roof and tramp it down. Later, if there was lumber available, a window would be cut in the cabin and glass installed. After the cabin was up, cracks between the logs were chinked with a mixture of mud and lime, with dry grass to bind it together. The furniture consisted of a handmade table made from whatever was handy, a double bunk bed, and some shelves for the grub.

When the cabin was completed they went prospecting—likely for the summer. If no values were found, they would pack up their donkeys and head for a warmer climate for the winter, returning the following spring for another try at looking for a strike.

One interesting party was given a pack train of burros in the White Cross area. There were several buildings in the later years that were abandoned, leaving old newspapers and large cans of old bacon grease. The pack train of Jumbo Peak and his brother were packing ore for the area to the smelter at Durango; one evening Jumbo said that he was going to have a party for his donkeys. He melted up the old grease and scattered the newspapers outside the cabin and then poured the grease on the papers. The burros went after the papers and feast. The Peak brothers had 40 good-sized jacks in their train; each one had a name and knew it. All the saddles were labeled, with the jack's name painted on the front. When it was time for saddling the jacks, his name was called and he was supposed to come and have his saddle on. Some of 'em came and some didn't, but when one did not come the dogs were told to get him, speaking the name of the jack. The dogs knew the jacks as well as the Peaks did and went after the jack in dead earnest, one dog running at the jack's head and the other at his heels. Soon he was ready for the saddle. The jacks did not forget this lesson. A good-sized jack would be loaded with three hundred pounds or according to the trip, whether it was short, steep, or a long trip. The Peak brothers packed two hundred tons of coal from Animas Forks to the Bon Homme Mine at White Cross in 1902. The first jack to be loaded with sacked coal was the leader of the train, a small jack that would follow the route once he was over it. The jacks were turned loose with their load and when all were packed the men mounted their horses and rode up the trail after them headed for the mine. The lead jack knew that if he went directly to the Bon Homme Mine three miles from Animas Forks he would be relieved of his load as soon as he arrived there. The men at the mine around the power house, seeing the jacks as they came in, would untie the ropes and unload them; then the burros could eat and rest until all of them arrived with their loads and then they headed back to the Forks for another load.

From 1900 to 1905 the Pittsburg Mining Company operated the Wyoming Mine on upper Henson Creek between New Port Basin and the Frank Hough Mine. Dave Bales packed in the supplies and coal for the boiler with a train of burros. The trail from Rose's Cabin was mostly above timberline and the snow in the winter was deep and always drifting. E. W. Creel estimated that it cost the company $10,000 to keep the trail open. This was the first attempt to pack to the mine in the winter. After this the supplies were laid in for the entire winter before snows came. Later when the Golconda operated their mine in Hurricane Basin they had a pack train of mules and trips were made from Rose's cabin to the mine. Mules were much more adapted to following a trail in the snow than were the donkeys, as their legs were longer and they would take better care of themselves than did their parents. The lead mule would put his nose to the trail where it was covered over with drifted snow and smell out where he put his feet. A burro would become stubborn and sulky while a mule never went anywhere he was not sure of his footing. The mules also could carry a larger load than the smaller jack.

After the pack trains came the wagon roads and four- and six-horse teams—also mule teams with jerk lines. After the arrival of these trains into Lake City in 1889 the transportation to and from the mines had to be done by teams and wagons until the arrival of the trucks, which was not until 1920 in this area. Then most of the roads were not wide enough for the operation of trucks and some wagons were still used.

Packtrain of Jumbo Peak.

STRIKE AT THE UTE-ULAY AND
HIDDEN TREASURE

On March 14, 1899, a strike of the miners began at Lake City, Hinsdale County, Colorado, or to be more exact, at the village of Henson, which is three miles from Lake City. Two mines were affected, the Ute-Ulay and the Hidden Treasure. The Auric Mining Company leased and operated the Ute and Ulay Mine and Mill, in which about 100 men were employed, of whom about forty were Italians. The Hidden Treasure Mining and Milling Company employed about the same number of men, with about the same proportion of foreigners. The Italians were members of a union of the Western Federation of Miners which had been organized only a few months previously. Some of the Americans were also members of this union. The cause of the strike was the requirement that all single men in this employ should board at the company boarding house. The Italians refused to comply. The Americans were unaware of the disturbance until the day shifts started to work on March 14 and were met by Italians armed with rifles. Not a man was allowed to enter the mine. Those who tried to return to work were beaten by the Italians who threatened to shoot them.

The discovery was made that the State Armory at Lake City had been broken into and arms and ammunition—50 Springfield rifles and 1,000 rounds of ammunition—had been removed. Investigators showed that the Italians had purchased nearly all the Winchester rifles and other firearms on sale in the town.

Lieutenant W. C. Blair of the local militia, Company A, Second Infantry, National Guard of Colorado, telegraphed to Colonel George F. Gardner, Inspector General at Denver that the Armory had been broken into and received orders from Gardner to put the sheriff and officers onto the burglary and to arrest all concerned in taking the arms and ammunition and to keep him advised by wire. Col. Gardner left for Lake City March 14. Sheriff James Deck and deputy went to the mines but accomplished nothing. He closed all the saloons at Henson. The Italians refused to submit to the arrest of any of their number nor allow any of the Americans to return to work. On March 15 eleven Italians submitted to arrest and upon the signing of peace bonds were released. W. C. Clark, secretary of the local union was arrested and charged with breaking into the Armory and taking the arms and ammunition. The sheriff visited Henson March 15 and was convinced that the strikers meditated violence. He telegraphed to Governor Charles Thomas, "I hereby request aid of the State Militia in quelling rioting." Governor Thomas ordered four companies of infantry and two companies of cavalry—326 men and officers—to the scene. Dr. Cuneo, the Italian consul, also arrived on the scene that he might plead with his countrymen to lay down their arms. Captain Macary, who was in charge of the troops, was reinforced at Pueblo with Adj. General Barnum. The riot was soon squelched but the mines refused to hire any more Italians. Sam Nicholson was superintendent of the Ute-Ulay and P. C. McCarthy of the Treasure. The troops were withdrawn March 20 and work resumed.

Clark, who had been arrested, was a former member of the Pitkin Guards, and knew where the guns were. However the guns were never recovered.

Ute and Ulay and tramway.

NEWSPAPERS

The *Silver World*, the first paper published on the Western Slope of Colorado, made its first appearance June 19, 1875. It was headed "Silver World, issued every Saturday by the Lake City Printing Co., H. M. Woods, Editor."
 The introductory paragraph, as copied from the editorial page, stated: "We Dip Our Colors To The Public. To supply the need of the San Juan Country for a paper which might be its exclusive representative, the Silver World has been inaugurated, and now makes its bow to the public. It is customary for all new aspirants for journalistic honors and favors to make a multitude of promises. We have none to make further than we shall endeavor to carry out the design above stated. ... Believing that all our miners and prospectors are fully supplied with religious reading, we shall preach no sermons. Thus we will have nothing pressing upon our time or space to prevent our giving full and complete reports from this and adjacent mining districts. These are the colors under which we shall sail, and having dipped them to the public, we nail them to the mast. Reader, if you want to sail with us, the fare is three dollars for a yearly trip."
 Another part of the paper describes the difficulties under which the paper was started.
 "Less than two weeks ago the material for this office was just delivered from the freight office. In the short space of eleven days we have laid the type, put together the stands and racks, set up the press and set forth our first edition. It may be thought that if we had taken a little more time it would have made the paper a little more readable, but we were anxious that it should make its appearance as early as possible in order to keep pace with the energy displayed by other citizens. Our material, with the exception of the press, is entirely new.
 Our office is a log cabin built on a sand bed, and is, in places, four or five inches deep with fine dust. For the press and stands we had to sink mudsills in order to make a solid foundation. The roof is of saplings covered with mud, and dirt sifts

down upon us in a never-ending shower. We lack all the conveniences and many of the things usually considered necessities in a printing office. But still we are happy, and present this issue with some satisfaction. Although it may not be all that could be desired, it is all that could be expected under the circumstances."

By August 1875, it had grown enough to move from the log cabin to the second story of the Finley building and in May, 1876, moved to a building on Third Street between Silver and Gunnison Avenue. In September, 1876, Woods sold his interest in the paper to Henry C. Olney. In 1877 the old Washington handpress was discarded and replaced with a new Campbell press.

In 1878 Henry C. Olney became the sole owner and editor of the paper. William Harbottle joined the staff of the paper as associate editor and traveled all over the San Juan area gathering news. He was succeeded by Frank Parmalee. In August, 1885, Olney leased the paper to A. R. Pelton, after which it changed hands a number of times. One of the editors was Gid Proper, former husband of Mrs. George Gardner, who married Lt. Governor Gardner while he was in office.

In 1887 Walter Mendenhall ran the paper, changing the name to "The Hinsdale *Phonograph*."

In 1887 Harry Woods and Thomas Reynolds started another paper which they called the *San Juan Crescent*, but there was not enough business in town to support two papers; it soon failed.

In 1880 James Downey, believing the town could support a paper devoted to mining interest, started the *Mining Register*. It lasted for five years, the last issue being published in 1885. Downey went to Montrose and started the *Montrose Register*. In 1890 a group of businessmen started the Lake City Printing and Publishing Company. They were Dr. D. S. Hoffman, O. H. Knight, W. J. Furse, and D. A. Farrell. The editor was a Denver man named A. R. Arbuckle. They called it the *Lake City Times*. It did not last long.

In 1901 Cris C. Wright started The *San Cristobal*, a magazine, published quarterly, but it lasted only a few years.

In 1898 O. H. Knight joined the names of *The Lake City Times* and The *Silver World*. Several years before, Walter Mendenhall had started the *Lake City Phonograph*, which John Uglo took over in 1895, and ran it until 1909. At that time Walter Mendenhall again took it over but soon gave it up.

W. C. Blair again started the *Silver World* in 1908, which he edited for two years when Harry Baker took over and ran it until 1913.

C. V. Kinney ran the Lake City Times from 1908 until 1914. Blair hired different editors on the *Silver World*, taking it over again about 1925 and carried it on until 1938. Walter Mendenhall edited the paper for him for a few years and Mathew Kinney, son of C. V. Kinney, worked there from 1920 to 1921.

After the last issue of the *Silver World* in 1938, the town did not have a paper until 1946 when Ollin Wineland started the *Lake City Tribune*, having resigned from the faculty of Western State College at Gunnison to establish it. His brother, H. L. Wineland, was the editor and Mrs. Carolyn Wright (author) was the associate editor. This paper continued until 1948. Mrs. Wright, who had been writing a Lake City column for the *Gunnison News Champion* since 1933, continued her work there, and that, with a column for the *Gunnison Globe* written by Mrs. Eileen Rawson, and later by Alice Green, are the only sources of Lake City news.

Hidden Treasure Mill, Office, and Bunkhouse.

POST OFFICES

The Lake City post office was established in 1875 and was serviced by stage from Del Norte whenever the stages made their trips. Later the service was from Gunnison by stage, until 1889 when the D & RG narrow gauge railroad came in from Sapinero. This service lasted until October of 1933. When the railroad was abandoned by order of the Public Utilities Commission, temporary service was given by Star Route from Sapinero by way of the Sapinero Mesa. In 1932 Star Route was established from Gunnison to Lake City and it is still in operation (1962).

The first postmaster was Stephen A. Dole, who served from 1875 to 1880. At that time the post office was located on Gunnison Avenue opposite what is now the Lake Garage. Dole was followed by A. Simmons, who served from 1881 to 1885, and the location was one door north of the first post office. Herman Leuders was the third postmaster, serving from 1886 to 1890; during his term the post office was located in the William Patterson building adjacent the Old American House on Gunnison Avenue. R. Herriman followed, serving from 1891 to 1896 in the post office between Second and Third Streets, the location of the Women's Club from 1940. George Gardner, at the Whitmore Building on Third Street between Silver and Gunnison, was another of the old-time postmasters. Steinbeck was the postmaster in 1892 to 1902. The location of the post office at this time was in the Avery building, just north of the Old Pueblo House on Silver Street. Mr. Steinbeck installed the first modern post office fixtures in this area. The fixtures were of sold oak, built in sections so that they could be placed to conform with any floor space. There were 218 combination boxes including four large drawers, a money order window and two delivery windows. These fixtures were used by all the postmasters until they were replaced in 1959 by the post office department. Before this the fixtures had to be furnished at the expense of the postmasters and no rental was allowed the owner.

Present Lake City post office. Photo courtesy of Mrs. Ruby Colopy.

First Lake City post office. Photo courtesy of Mrs. Ruby Colopy.

First post office at Capitol City. Wright picture.

Post office at White Cross when H. E. Wright was postmaster. Photo courtesy of Mrs. Margaret Witherite.

Last post office at Capitol City. Photo courtesy of Mrs. Margaret Witherite.

W. H. Ogle was the postmaster in 1902-1906 and at that time the post office was located on the corner of Third and Silver Street in the front part of the Lake City Drug Store, which was later the Hoffman Store. In 1907 Alex Harvinson served as the postmaster at the northwest corner of Third and Silver Street adjoining the Whinnery Store. His term ended in 1914. In October of 1914 C. E. Wright took over the position at the location and it remained there until 1920 when it was moved to the south part of the Bank Building. It was again moved in 1926 to the Stone Building (now the Log Cabin Inn). When W. O. Snowden became postmaster in 1935 the location of the post office was changed to the Avery Building, opposite the Lake City Drug Store on Silver Street. In 1938 it was moved back to the location where it had been under Harvinson and Wright. Following Snowden's termination in 1941, Ethel Lewis became postmistress and the location was the building south of the Stone Bank Building. Alice Green became the next postmistress, in 1952, at the old Pueblo House (now the Forbes antique shop). In 1953 Ruby Colopy took over the position and has served as postmistress until the present time (1963) at the location adjoining the Lone Pine Apartments on the east side of Gunnison Avenue between Second and Third Streets.

A flood in 1921 interrupted the railroad mail service to Lake City from Sapinero and the Golconda pack train under the leadership of Harry Kearns temporarily took over the duties. In 1915 on the first to the tenth of March there was no mail service into or out of Lake City due to heavy snow and slides in the Black Canyon south of Sapinero, as the train was stalled after breaking a plow while attempting to clear the tracks from Gunnison west to Montrose. After repairs were made the crew started from Sapinero to clear the tracks into Lake City. At the Chas. Carr Ranch, Madera, there was a water tank where the engines stopped for their water supply. At this tank there was a spur track where the switch was left open and the two engines with the snow plow got on the spur track and soon came to the end. The snow was so deep that the end was not visible and they ran off the track and out onto the flat about two hundred feet. It took some time before the engines could again head for Lake City. As a result there was no mail for ten days.

Named after J. E. Carson, who located on the eastern slope of the Continental Divide, there were some cabins. Some of the really old cabins are still standing along the ridge at the mouth of Wager Canyon. The camp of Carson was established in 1897 and the post office was serviced by horseback during the summer and in snowshoes during the winter. Service was discontinued in 1905. During the time which this post office was active John Murphy carried the mail on his pony George and the postmaster was P. Carrol.

Childs Park had no service although a Mr. Stephen always had stamps for sale and letters could be mailed from there under the postmark and sent to Lake City. This office was discontinued in 1918.

The Lake Shore Post Office, established in 1895 and discontinued in 1906, with its postmasters Doc Bothwell and Mrs. Cameron, was served by Star Route which came from Lake City. This same service also served Sherman and White Cross. The service was daily except Sunday and was curtailed during winter months.

The Henson post office, which was named after Captain George A. Henson, was located four miles from Lake City at the Ute & Ule mines. It was established in 1894 and its postmasters were Duffy, Meyers, and Lena Meyers. The service was discontinued in 1910. It, too, was serviced by Star Route from Lake City.

Capitol City, 10 miles south of Lake City on Henson Creek, named by Mr. Lee who had hopes of this site becoming the capitol of the state, was the site of the Capitol City post office. This office was established in 1898 and discontinued in 1920. Its postmasters were William Owens, Margaret Witherite, Mrs. Buskirk and Ben Gionneau. This was the only other post office in the county having money order service. Incorporated in 1879, Capitol City was also the only other incorporated town in Hinsdale County.

All of the post offices in the drainage of the Lake Fork River were served from the Lake City post office. Other post offices within the county were served from the nearest offices, such as Hermit from Creede, Cathedral from Powderhorn, and Debs from Pagosa Springs. Some of the factors for establishment and service were the number of patrons to be served, the time of the year—winter or summer—and the road conditions. The only offices to have daily service were the Lake City, Henson, and Capitol City offices; the other offices had service only every other day or twice weekly in the summertime only. In the early days, wherever there was a mine operating such as Carson or White Cross, the winter supplies were all laid in for the entire winter months and contacts with the outside were only made when it was necessary and then by snowshoes.

H. E. Wright, in his diary of 1877, described Burrows Park as the area out of Campbell's Hill to the mouth of the American Basin. There was not a camp known as Burrows Park. The first camp in the White Cross area was Argentum, named for argentiflour ores which were found in that location. J. H. Sloan built his cabin there in 1876. The camp had two stores, three hotels, a blacksmith shop, and twelve cabins along the street. I can remember the blacksmith's shop and the canvas belt that was used to raise the bulls with a windlass to shoe them. This camp was on the flat north of what is now called Cooper Creek; about one half mile south of the camp was the first sawmill, almost opposite Stoney Creek where the river flows over the cliffs. Water power was used and one handhewn log can still be seen at the top of the cliffs where the mill stood. Tim Clawson operated the hotel and store where the mail was delivered. The mail was addressed to Argentum, Colorado, via Lake City, and this post office was located 20 miles south of Lake City on the Lake Fork.

The second camp in this district was named after Tellurium, an ore which was found there. This camp was located about two miles south of Argentum. The buildings were scattered over about one quarter of a mile, on both sides of the road where the line fence now crosses the road. Five adjoining cabins were the main part of this camp. One quarter of a mile east of Cleveland Gulch, two of the buildings stood near the south of this gulch and the remains of a fireplace can still be seen. Also at this time there was built the Gunnison Mill. The foundation can be seen at the site of the Gunnison lode. There was no regular service to or from this camp. The post office was established by J. C. Priddy in 1877 and his assistant was H. E. Wright.

The next camp which had a post office was White Cross. It was established in 1885 and discontinued in 1907. H. E. Wright was the first postmaster. He served until 1904 when J. H. Sloan was appointed. There was mail service during the winter of 1901 and during the following two summers there was daily mail service to and from White Cross. Before this, and afterwards, the office was closed in the winter months and reopened when the roads were passable in the spring. Mining in the winter was limited and the miners laid their supplies in ahead of time and left the camp only on snowshoes.

Paid by the miners at a dollar a month, I delivered mail on horseback all the way from White Cross to within two miles of Animas Forks. Most of the mail was letters; however, there were also some papaers and a few packages which were limited to four pounds. There was no parcel post. There were over three hundred receiving mail from White Cross during 1902.

Sherman was named for F. S. Sherman and establisblished in 1897. Homer Harrington was the postmaster and the service was via Star Route from Lake City. This service was discontinued in 1905 and the remaining cabins received mail only when the stage stopped.

WAR SAVING AND THRIFT STAMPS

In 1918 Uncle Sam put on sale, to supplement the War Bonds, government war savings and thrift stamps through the post offices. Unlike the war bonds, there was no quota for states or counties. Chairman of the 16th district of Colorado—consisting of Hinsdale, San Juan, Ouray, and Montrose counties—Chas J. Moynihan, offered a loving-cup for the county selling the most stamps. The amount of sale was judged by the population. Postmaster Wright organized the drive in Hinsdale county, and with the cooperation of the whole county, succeeded in placing a war saving stamp in every home in the county. The sum of $26,000 was raised through the sale of thrift and war saving stamps, the largest sale in the district. A celebration was held in the City Hall, where C. J. Moynihan awarded the loving cup to Hinsdale County. After presentation of the cup, Mr. Moynihan recited "In Flanders Field Where Poppies Grow," in honor of our war dead. The celebration was finished by all joining in a well-attended dance.

This cup was in the Lake City post office from the time of presentation until 1935 when Mr. Wright left the post office department, at which time it was taken to the Office of the Hinsdale County Clerk where it can now be seen.

La Belle Tunnel at White Cross.

ROADS

Many of the present roads are along the general route or have been changed. The first road up the Lake Fork went up Crooke's Hill from the Texan Resort straight up the hill, then along the present site to Shot Gun Point where the road went above the point and came into the flat below Vicker's Dude Ranch. From the ranch, the road followed the edge of the meadow on the west side, leaving the meadow at the south end and over the rise across Silver Coin Gulch, dropping down to the edge of the river, which was followed to Argenta Falls where it came up to the present road. The general direction was followed to the bridge, almost where the present bridge now stands. After crossing the bridge it continued around the lake on the east side then climbing the hill to the first cabins on the east side of the lake, crossing Dinty Moore Gulch, down to the edge of the lake where the government cabins are. Some of the old road was visible before the Paddock Dam was put in. The road from the government cabins went along the shore line of the lake and then over the hill along where the camp sites are. Then it dropped down to the river at the upper bridge. From here the road was on the east side of the river to the seven-mile bridge, where it crossed the river to the west side of the Lake Fork, up and over the Clawson Mesa, down to the river opposite the Clawson Ranch, where it was necessary to ford the river as there was no bridge. Skirting the meadow, it continued between the buildings and the river and across Rough Creek, over the rise to the eastern part of the Reese Richart Ranch (now the Porter Ranch) and along the edge of the meadow toward the ranch house where the road passed between the house and the meadow and then up the rise, along the river to where the present road comes out east of Childs' Park Bridge. The road stayed on the east side of the river until Bent Creek, where there was a bridge. The road went over the rise and down to the river on the west side, continuing along the very edge of the stream and across Mud Mill Flat, which is now a part of the Bryant Ranch. It continued on the west of the river to Sherman, fording the Lake Fork over the flat where the old Fox Farm was, and then toward the mouth of Cottonwood Gulch where the climb began on the east side of the Lake Fork toward White Cross. This road was very steep and only wide enough for the wagon wheels. Every once in a while there was a turn-out where teams could pass. The road continued to Corwin Gulch where there was another bridge, bringing the road to the west side of the river. It continued over Campbell Hill and down again to the edge of the river, following it up to Silver Creek. (It was between the present road and the river.) It crossed Silver Creek by bridge, went on past the Great Ohio cabins, to the lower dump of the Ohio workings and up the steep hill presently in use. Parts of this old road bed can be seen just below the road now used. The road then came through the main street of the real old town of Argentum (named after the argentiferous galena found there by the first settlers). The bridge crossing the Cooper Creek was about fifty feet to the east of where the present bridge crosses the stream, going straight up the hill from the town. About two hundred yards above this hill the road did not follow the one presently used, but was to the west and can still be seen above the road. The old road joined the present one almost at Pass Creek, (sometimes called Stony) continuing on almost the same road bed now in use to the old site of the White Cross post office. From here the road at present is almost the same as years ago, passing the site of the old town of Tellurium (named after the gold ore) over the Stony Wash from Cleveland Gulch, past the Gunnison Mill site, and skirting the eastern foot at Edith Mountain. There are some changes in the road from this point to the top of the Bon Homme Hill. The present road is nearer Edith Mountain and the old road is near the creek. This road was very steep toward the Bon Homme Mine, so the now-traveled road was constructed higher up from the bottom of the main gulch. After passing the Bon Homme Mine, the road followed nearer the river than the present one and crossed the stream from Rainbow Basin and the Tobasco Mill. Nearer the main river, climbing the almost bare rocks to a point about two hundred yards from the switchback in the American Basin, where the old road turned off to the left and climbed at a very steep rate north, crossing below the Tobasco Mill. This was at the same point as the present road. Instead of turning right as the now-traveled road, the old road went straight up the hill toward the Tobasco Mill, then followed the stream up Rainbow Basin to the top of the range or Cinnamon Pass. The present road is on the hillside on much higher ground than the old one and is not nearly so steep. The old road did not cross the divide into Cinnamon Basin at the same place as the later one does as it took off to the right and crossed the Continental Divide higher up near the little lake at the top. Going down Cinnamon Pass there were many changes in the road, but they all continued in the same direction toward Animas Forks down toward the lower end of the Basin where the present road now swings around the hill coming into the road from Engineer Mountain above the Forks. The old road made a switchback and followed the stream down to the Animas River, where it joined the road below the Forks. It continued on the north side of the Animas River almost to the town of Eureka, where the road crossed on the log bridge, on into the town and to the old Balloon or Baseball Grounds (I played ball here in 1908), past the Hamlet Mill, the Kittymack Mill, through the town of Howardsville, past the old Hundred Mill, then across the Animas by log bridge and from there on into Silverton. The present road from Animas Forks to Eureka is the old railroad grade used and built by the Silverton Northern Railroad. One of the little old narrow gauge engines could only push one freight car or pull it from Eureka to Animas Forks. Going down with two cars loaded with concentrates from the Gold Prince Mill at the Forks one engine could not hold the cars back and they finally stopped at the Kittymack Mill almost one mile below Eureka—with no casualties.

This railroad grade was built in 1901 by the Silverton Northern Railroad, employing the whole tribe of Navajo Indians, who lived in their native style on the hillside around the town. It was hand work with teams and scrapers. I made several trips from White Cross to see the Indians at work. The squaws on very small ponies with papooses strapped on their backs would travel as far as Sherman from the Forks and return the same day. Anything loose was, or should have been, fastened down; if not, it would follow the Indians back to camp.

The road from Animas Forks to Engineer Mountain has been changed so many times that now one does not know just what road they are traveling, the old one or the new one. But the general direction and route is used with the exception being the road from Denver Ridge to and over Engineer Mountain did not go near the Frank Hough mine as it now does, but went over the lower ridge at the north and came into the Henson Creek upper country through Newport and the lower Hurricane Basins, past the Chicago Tunnel. The road from the upper part of Mineral Creek, now Poughkeepsie, was constructed many years later. This road did not really cross Engineer Mountain until after going through the head of Bear Creek over Engineer and into the upper part of Frank Hough Basin and then down to Rose's Cabin. The next road from Lake City to Lake Shore (Lake San

Christobal) is the present one traveled, having been widened and ditched. After reaching the foot of the lake the second road was along the west side of the lake and followed the shore line. None of this road can be seen because when the Paddock dam was built, it raised the lake and covered the old road. The road continued up the canyon above the lake on the west side of the river. The road now used remains the same to just above the Clawson Ranch (now the Red Cloud Ranch) where Rough Creek joins the Lake Fork. The road went on the west side of the river to Child's Park, then crossed the bridge where it joined the present one. This road from Rough Creek to Child's Park was changed to the east side of the river, its present location, and continued to Sherman, where the road was built on the west side. Also the old road was changed below and above the Tobasco Mill to the present road, which is the fourth road. The third one was above Argenta Falls near the General Sherman across the portal dump of the Contention Mine, climbing above the lower Fleece Tunnel and along the hillside near the Heath cabin, and just west of Turtle Island cabin, where it joined the present one at Pioneer Point. This third road was built by A. E. Reynolds in 1901. Mr. Reynolds wanted to use water power from the lake for a plant under Argenta Falls. In order to do so, he could not utilize any water from the lake at the present level, but was granted permission to use any water stored above the lake level, so an earthen dam was proposed to be built to raise the lake level sixty feet. The third road was built to be above the shore line of the new lake. For unknown reasons the dam was not built. Evidence of the diversion ditch to change the river while the dam was under construction can be seen just below the bridge and between the road and the river. Many law suits were involved concerning the dam. Reynolds, who had a large interest in mining throughout the district became displeased with the outcome of these law suits and vowed that he would see the grass growing in the streets of Lake City. As a result he and his associates withdrew from Hinsdale County and I have seen the grass growing in the streets of Lake City.

The roads up Henson Creek have not varied much from the old ones. However, there were four bridges between Lake City and Fanny Fern Mill. About 50 feet from the turnoff to the county powder house, the first log bridge stood. The second log bridge was 100 feet up the canyon. The river was at that time on the west side of the park. Between the two bridges was the site of the famous beer gardens where the town enjoyed many social activities. The road now on the west side of the river, continued about one half mile to the third bridge. This one was also of log construction. Just across the river from this bridge was the cabin of the toll gate keeper and two hundred feet farther on was the fourth bridge, where the road crossed to the west side of the river just opposite the Fanny Fern Mill. It then continued up the river with little change until it reached El Paso Creek where the old road was nearer the river than is the present one. Above Capitol City, later the site of the Moro Mill, the road crossed the river to the east side, continuing along the flat and up Whitmore Hill and past the Whitmore Falls. Just above the falls where the water from Galena Basin enters the Lake Fork was a wooden bridge. Here the road crossed to the west side of the river and from here on to Rose's cabin the road was along the creek rather like the present one on the hillside. From Rose's cabin the road crossed to the east side again, under the Chicago Tunnel, into Hurricane Basin, through Newport Basin and over Engineer Mountain.

The generation of today goes to the stores for the needed material or supplies. But at the beginning of the settlement in Hinsdale County there were no stores to go to. Everything used had to be produced from natural resources or shipped in by freight from distant points. I believe that the first real necessity for beginning a town is lumber. There was abundant supply of native timber all around, so necessary parts for a saw mill were freighted in and set up for operation. In early 1876 there were two saw mills operating in Lake City and then came brick yards for the production of brick, which were made of local mud and clay burned in kilns located on the grounds. To make brick walls it was necessary to have lime and sand for mortar. Lime dykes were discovered and developed and sand was found in the nearby streams, so now wooden, brick and stone buildings could be built. When the Crooke's Smelter was brought in and set up for operation it was necessary to have fluxes, fuels, and iron ores to make the reduction of the ores possible. From the bricks now on hand charcoal kilns were constructed for charcoal to be used for fuel at the smelter and also for fuel in the blacksmith shops. Dykes from the already discovered lime were available. Iron beds were found and developed for use in the smelter. The largest of the iron beds was Wetterhorn on Wetterhorn Creek, from which the ore was freighted to the smelter at Crooke's Falls by ox teams and wagons. The object of the smelter was to reduce the metal to a refined product known as a mat. This mat was black in color and any special metal such as silver, gold, lead or copper was not visible to the eye, but all the values were in the mat. This mat was made into bars and shipped to a refinery for separation of the ores. There were several other reduction plants in the area such as the Ocean Wave at the north end of town, the Lee Smelter at Capitol City, and the Lixivation Works on the hill near the junction of Silver Street, Gunnison Avenue and the southern boundaries of the town.

The charcoal kilns previously mentioned were usually built on units of two or three, in the shape of a bee hive. These kilns were about sixteen feet in height and the same width, circular in construction, coming to a point at the top. The principal ones were located at Horse Park, Capitol City and north of town just below Blue Cut on the old Hugard Ranch; while all of the kilns are not standing there can be seen the circular bases of them, at Capitol City, across the stream, east of the bridge, passing the large pile of saw dust, about three hundred yards and the remains of the kilns can be viewed. One cannot see them until nearly up to them as the trees and foliage have almost concealed them. The ones in Horse Park can be reached by horseback, and the ones north of town can be seen from the very southern part of the San Juan Ranch from across the river. Later as the improved roads made the use of coal available from the Gunnison country, there was no use for charcoal.

Saw mills and brick yards were in the Sherman district. There was also a saw mill between Argentum and Tellurium in the Burrows Park area. This one was powered by water, while most of the other mills were operated by steam. One of the most interesting saw mills was in Sherman where lumber was sawed for the West End Mill (later known as the Black Wonder Mill). This saw mill was powered by a narrow gauge railroad engine running on rails. The saw was not stationary but mounted on the front of the engine; the log was fastened by dogs at the side of the tracks so that the saw was pushed through the log. All the other mills around here had a stationary saw and the carriage with the log was moved through the saw. All of the work in the development of the mines from 1875 to the late nineties was done by hand. The first powder used was black, which varied from the size of a kernal of corn down to about the same size as a grain of wheat. After this kind of explosive came the giant powder, then Hercules, Atlas, and Dupont. The first giant powder was very effective. It had to be soft for use. The powder would not stand cold weather and could not be exploded when frozen so the problem out in the hills was to keep it from freezing. This was done by several means, and it could not be exposed directly to fire as it would explode. Later types of explosives were marketed that would stand the cold and would not have to be kept from freezing. Also hand steel in various lengths and makes, Jessop, Canton and Swedish were used. Three quarters, seven eighths, and thirteen sixteenths were the most popular sizes used after the first hand steel of one inch. After hand steel came the machine steel, which was at first in the square steel, then hexigon, with cross bits, then rose bits and later single bits. Lights for the mines consisted inch. After hand steel came the machine steel, which was at first in the square steel, then hexigon, with cross bits, then rose bits and later single bits. Lights for the mines consisted of many types, the first of which was the lard oil lamp worn on the caps of the miners. While it burned there was a black smoke from the lamp and when the miner came out of the mine at night his face would be black as coal. Next came the candle. There were several kinds: tallow, granite, and paraffin. Then carbide lamps were used. They were almost as bad for the lungs as the lard oil lamps. As electricity became available, electric lamps were used.

Early-day horseback riding—side saddle. (left) Mrs. Homer Harrington, wife of Sherman postmaster, and (right) Mrs. George Gardner, wife of adjutant general.

AREAS AND MINES AROUND LAKE CITY

Outside the immediate vicinity of Lake City the mining activity was centered around the Burrows Park and Sherman areas. In 1876 there were two post offices, Argentum and Tellurium, with thirty mines in operation employing 200 men.
The first mill was built by the Gunnison Mines Company; this was gravity concentrates, powered by water taken from the river through a ditch and then flume to the mill with Pelton wheel and direct drive shaft in the mill, one table trommel screen and one jig. This mill was dismantled in 1895 and sold to the West End Company at Sherman which was then working the Black Wonder Mine. Road conditions hampered mining at this time as there were no roads except those which had been built by the miners themselves. Due to this condition and the lack of capital to develop the mines, the district became almost inactive until 1900 when White Cross became active. Mining again was resumed and there were 300 men receiving mail at the White Cross post office. The camp consisted of post office, store, saloon, hotel and boarding house, thirteen cabins, only two of which were of the town of Tellurium, two stables and two strings of pack animals. The principal mines were LaBelle, Bon Homme, Champion, Baltimore, Philadelphia, Great Ohio, Japanese, Isolde, and Premier. The Bon Homme and LaBelle both installed boilers and compressors, and the Champion and Great Ohio put in new boilers and hoists. All were steam plants as there was no electrical power available. The Tobasco Mill and aerial tramway were under construction, with water power plant at Sherman from where the three-wire line was run to the mill and mine. The Tobasco Company operated the mill only a very short time as the whole setup was a stock-selling scheme. After the mill was completed the only ones making any money from it were the promoters, while the stockholders were left holding worthless stock. This was one of others in the history of mining in Hinsdale County that helped to reduce mining in the county, as at one time the mention of Hinsdale County and mining to real mining men was immediately given

the cold shoulder. In 1906 I saw equipment at both mine and mill being packed away by anyone who wanted it, as there was no watchman on the property. Since 1905 there has been little or no real activity in this area, only miners who did their assessment work. The first and only powered mucking machine in the White Cross area and on the Lake Fork River as of 1952 was on the View of the Park lode.

    The Sherman district with the town of Sherman as the center was a lively camp as early as 1877 when the Black Wonder, George Washington, Minnie Lee, Come Up, Sterling, Smile of Fortune, Irish World, Adelaide, Monster and IXL mines were working. Men were hard to find to work in the mines as they were all looking for a mine of their own, and would work only when they were short of a grubstake. The Black Wonder employed the most men. Later, in 1895, the West End Mining and Milling Company built the first mill and a two-bucket jig back tram from the mine to the mill, the mill was a roaster to reclaim the gold from the ore which was not there. After the stockholders' money gave out the camp went down until in 1900 the Black Wonder mill was remodeled and new workings added on the dike. A large steam engine was installed in the mill, powered by steam, the boilers fired with cord wood cut from the nearby hills. The company money did not last as there was no return from the ores mined and milled and the camp again became inactive and only three old-timers were there for many years. They were John Gavin (Grey Eagle), Sam Robinson, and Bill Sweeney. In 1925 the Black Wonder Mine and Mill again became active, operating on stock sold by Chicago promoters. Many needed repairs on mine, mill, and houses were made and the Town of Sherman again looked good. A two-mile pipeline was built, hung by cables anchored in the cliffs, dropping one thousand feet to the Pelton wheel, where a modern electric plant was operated and produced power for the mine and mill as well as the town street lights. The town was cleaned up, the streets were graded and the houses were in good repair. Baseball equipment was purchased and Sherman had a baseball team with a playing field across the Lake Fork towards the mouth of Cottonwood. One interesting structure still remains of the pipeline, while the other pipeline has long been taken away. There still remains the suspension bridge across the gulch just below the road to White Cross, about one mile above Sherman. This cable bridge supported the wooden pipeline across the gulch and was erected in 1925 by George Vernon and B. N. Ramsey, but was not built in the early seventies as one picture has it dated.

In the early seventies Carson City was very active, the principal mines were on the eastern slope of the Continental Divide, just over the top going into West Lost Trail Creek. The most prominent were St. Jacobs, Maid of Carson, Blizzard, Bonanza, King, West Lost Trail Group, Raven, Silver Spray, Tobinson Group, Jess and others. Later the Carson post office was established in 1897 when C. F. Meek began operation on the Bachelor and George III. New equipment, buildings, boilers and hoist were installed and the wagon road was kept open all winter. This camp was active until 1902 when Col. Meek became interested in the Yule Marble Works and turned his interests to M. L. Childs. Since then no extensive mining has been done.

On the west shore of Lake Sam Christobal was the post office of Lake Shore. Around this camp were the mines which supported the camp. The principal mines operating were The Golden Fleece, Hiawasse, Black Crook, Contention, General Sherman, and many other smaller ones. The Golden Fleece built a mill below the Argenta Falls. Ore from the mine high up on Hotchkiss Mountain was hauled to the mill by team and wagon. Later after the completion of the crosscut tunnel, ore was only hauled from the portal of the crosscut to the mill. The mill dumped tailings into the stream and the Lake City water works was polluted. The Fleece had to build a ditch from their mill to the top of Crook Hill to divert tailings below the intake of the water works. A part of this ditch can still be seen between Vicker's Ranch and Shotgun Point. The Contention built a mill just below the portal of the tunnel, which was one of the stock schemes and did not produce. Remains of this promotion which has hampered mining in Hinsdale County can be viewed from the road just above Argenta Falls.

In 1935 the El Dorado Company leased the Fanny Fern Mine north of Lake City, building an aerial tramway and mill. After completion of the mill and tramway the company went into bankruptcy and another gravestone to legitimate mining was laid. Three miles farther up Henson Creek from Lake City was the Hidden Treasure Mine and mill with aerial tramway from the mine to the mill. This company successfully operated from the start. The power was from water through a pipeline to the mill where a Pelton wheel generated power for the dynamo and electricity which operated the mill and the mine. None of the buildings are to be seen at present. However, the cement dam is still in place, but now filled with wash.

About one mile above the Hidden Treasure is the famous Ute and Ulay. Since the early eighties when the Crooke

Brothers owned and operated this ground, it has been the leading producer and employed the most men of any mine in this district. During boom days of any period the Ute was in operation and when this mine was not operating there was not much activity in the mines. The most interesting mode of transportation was the tramway from the upper workings of the Ute to the mill. This consisted of three tram cars fastened together, running on mine rails laid on the ground, extending up the steep hillside. Three cars loaded at the upper terminal would pull three empty cars up the hill. This was a gravity operation controlled by hand brake on the six-foot drum at the top terminal. The ore was unloaded into a bin in the mill below. This tramway was abandoned when the crosscut was completed. Power for mine and mill was from water and steam. In 1901 the Aurie Mining and Milling Company rebuilt the mill and installed the most modern steam compressor and engine the town had seen at that time. There was only one other plant like this and it was in Leadville, Colorado. This plant operated many years and is still at the original location in the power house. Anyone interested in machinery should see this huge plant as it is worth the effort to see. In 1925 a new flotation mill was erected and also a cement dam. The Ute and Ulay and the Hidden Treasure were combined under one name in 1940. In 1952 a new flotation mill was erected and also a cement dam. In 1952 the mill was again remodeled and the property was only active until 1953; since then there has been no work at the Ute.

Another property on Henson Creek with a mill was the Lellie, located eight miles from Lake City. The mill operated by electricity from water power out of Nellie Creek. Although the company did operate at a profit for a while, the mill was not the solution to their problem.

In the Capitol City area there were many mines that operated successfully. There were only three with mills. The Hannah Company erected a mill and tramway one mile above Capitol City and also a hydro-electric plant for the production of electric power. Ore from the Moro mine was milled at the Hannah also. Ore from the Highland Chief came by jig-back tram to the road from where it was hauled by wagon to the Hannah Mill. About 1930 the mill was dismantled. Another early property operating with a mill was the Yellow Medicine. This mill was of the very early type and only separated the ore by gravity. Some good ore was shipped from there, but the property has not operated for many years.

Another eyesore for the county was the erection of a mill at the Gullic Vulcan mines in North Henson. After the money was spent for the mill, which was modern, there was no money for development and the mill and buildings were dismantled less than five years after being built.

In 1901 the Henson Creek Lead Mining Company built a mill on their property. They also built a hydroelectric plant on the flat between the Moro Mill and Whitmore Falls, with a pipeline from Henson Creek at Boulder Gulch to the Pelton water wheel at the power plant. Their transmission line was about four miles. Operation of this plant and mill was of short duration and the property has not operated for many years. The electric plant has long been dismantled.

The Palmetto property also had a mill of the early type and shipments from there were of high grade. Other mines in the upper Henson Creek were Frank Hough, Wyoming, Dolly Varden, Varden Belle, Bob Ingersol, Dewey, Newport, Kentucky Boy, Independence, and many others from which ore was shipped but not developed into producing mines.

Lake City train on high bridge.

THE RAILROAD

The D&RG Railroad surveyed a proposed grade into Lake City in 1882, and a part of this grade was made; however, the work stopped and the road was not completed until 1889. In 1885, due to cost of transportation for supplies into and out of Lake City, local interests took up the matter of building their own railroad to Gunnison. At that time the railroad agreed to complete the line to Lake City. The first engine on the regular run to Lake City was #58, with Engineer Pete J. Ready and Conductor Hugh Gallagher. These two old-timers remained on this run from Sapinero until 1910 when both of these men acquired, by seniority, the Montrose-Grand Junction run. The runs of Lake City and Montrose were considered tops on the third division as both were daylight runs and the men could be at home with their families. Many of the other runs kept the men away from the families. Ready and Gallagher were on the Montrose run when they retired.

The service was from Lake City round trip to Sapinero where connection was made with a west-bound narrow gauge train from Salida to Montrose where the tracks were of broad gauge. The train left Lake City at 8 a.m. and traveled the 36 miles to Sapinero in three hours, where it waited until 3 p.m. for the train from the west from Montrose and then returned to Lake City, arriving there at 6 p.m.

The Currecanti Dam below Sapinero, now under construction, when completed will cover Sapinero and the lower Lake Fork River with three hundred feet of water, so the Lake Fork canyon will not be visible at the junction with the Gunnison River, where there were three bridges located just under the present steel bridge. One bridge was the highway bridge across the Lake Fork of the Gunnison River, next to it was the railroad bridge across the Lake Fork River, followed by a railroad bridge of the Lake City train. All of these bridges were within one hundred feet of each other.

Construction of the railroad into Lake City was not easy. There were many bridges to build and heavy grades made through solid rock. All of the rock work was done by hand and churn drills. There was no giantpowder or dynamite for explosives such as we now have. The old black powder was used and grades were not made by cats and cans, but rather by horse- and mule-drawn scrapers and fresnos. Then the ballast was hauled in by slips. Between Sapinero and Lake City there were ten bridges, four water tanks, two section station houses for the repair crews and stops along the line were Youmans, now the Ute Trail Ranch; Spruce, now the Lowell Carr Ranch; Madera, now the Charles Carr Ranch. The sections were Youman, 12 miles north of Lake City and Barnum, two miles down the canyon from the Charles Carr Ranch. The water tanks were a necessity, as all of the engines were of the steam type. Coal was used for fuel and the lights in the coaches were the swinging kerosene lamps. Some of these were stationary, but most of them were hung from the ceiling so that they could swing, as the tracks were not all smooth and the coaches would sway from side to side. For many years the railroad company retained a watchman at the High Bridge, which is eight miles north of Lake City. He lived in a house on the north side of the bridge and after each train went over the bridge he would patrol the high bridge and also the one at Elk Creek to prevent any sparks from setting the wooden bridges on fire. The tops of the bridges were later covered with rock surfacing so that the sparks could not cause a fire. It was at this time that the watchman, Mr. Bailey, was put out of a job. There were three service crews on the thirty six-mile run to Sapinero. The crew at Lake City maintained the first twelve miles to Norman and the Youman crew took care of the twelve miles, leaving the remaining twelve miles in the care of the Barnum crew. The worst part of maintaining the roadbed in the winter was the ice freezing in the tracks. This ice had to be picked out by hand. The snow was not such a problem, as they had snow and rotary plows to clear the tracks. Only when the snow was very heavy, and each part of the track had to wait its turn for the plows, would the snow cause trouble. On one occasion the crew was ready to depart from the station for their daily run with Pete Ready and Hugh Gallagher on duty as usual. Gallagher said, "Are you ready, Pete?" who replied, "No, but I am Pete Ready, let her go Gallagher." They left the station, but encountered snow in the cut east of the Ocean Wave mill. Pete thought that he could leave the coach and train at Fifth Street and make a run through the snow with the engine, which he attempted. He

First engine of the D&RG off the track in snow. Old Ocean Wave Mill in background.

backed up the track so that he could get a good run at the drifted snow and opened the throttle, the black smoke roaring from the smokestack. After crossing the bridge, he hit the snow and the engine began to groan and finally stopped. The snow piled on the track behind the engine and the packed snow was in front of the engine. Pete could not move the engine either way. He remained there for two days as the section crews shoveled out the engine.

Another amusing incident in the life of Pete as engineer was when he came into town one evening, whistling for the station one mile out of town as usual and pulled into the station. As he drew to a stop, he turned around to see if the coach was at the right point to come to a full stop, but he did not have any train. As usual, there were several people to see the train come in and they couldn't help but wonder what had happened to the rest of the train. Pete, however, realized what had happened. He opened the throttle and went around the loop heading out of town to find his lost train. Just after the track crossed High Bridge there was quite a heavy grade up the river to about Stony Gulch just north of the VC Ranch. It was on this grade that the train had come loose from the tender. The brakeman had tightened the hand brake when he realized what had happened—which was the only possible thing that he could do until Mr. Pete came back after them. Soon Pete came barreling back down the tracks; the coupling was made fast to the train and they again headed for Lake City. This incident cost Pete, who was a very good fellow, a good many laughs and some cigars.

After crossing the third bridge where Highway 50 crosses the river to the east side of the Lake Fork, the train traveled on this side of the river until it reached Spruce near the Lowell Carr Ranch where it crossed to the west side. The next bridge was a higher trestle at Elk Creek, one mile south of the Youman station (Ute Trail). It then continued up the Lake Fork to the highest bridge, which, of course, was High Bridge, eight miles north of Lake City. This trestle was two hundred feet long and one hundred feet high. The bridges were all constructed with 10 x 10 and 12 x 12 (inch) sawed timber. In 1921 the bridge was pushed out of alignment by the water backing up behind it with debris and logs. If it had not been for the work of men from Lake City, the bridge would likely have been washed out. The original bridge footing was driven piling. This had to be replaced after the flood, in 1921, with cement footing across the river; some of these cement footings are still visible. After crossing the high bridge, the line was on the east side of the canyon and remained on this side until the next bridge, one mile south of the Baker ranch, and then crossed to the west side, about one quarter mile upstream. The next bridge crossed the river about opposite the TCM tunnel to the east side. At Larson Creek the bridge crossed the river to the west side on up through the J. C. Bell ranch, which is now the Valley View ranch, and the Greenfield (now San Juan) ranch to the next bridge at the Blue Cut, crossing to the east side one mile from the Lake City Station. The last bridge crossed the river between Sixth and Eighth Streets. This was the longest and the last bridge on the line. At the Lake City Station, consisting of a building two hundred feet long and fifty feet in width, with a platform of three-inch plank around the building, were two- and four-wheel hand-drawn trucks used to load and unload the freight from the cars. Side tracks were on each side of the depot where cars could be spotted for freight. The loop between the depot and the river was used to reverse the direction of the engine and train. There was a roundhouse in the center, where the engine was stabled and refueled. There was office equipment and telegraph instruments, a ticket counter and, of course, the pot-bellied stove for heat. Adjoining the office was the waiting room, which was 20 x 24 feet; oak benches surrounded the walls and another large pot-bellied stove was in the center of the room. There were side tracks extending from the depot north from Second Street to Sixth Street and also south from the depot to Henson Creek. These side tracks were used for loading and unloading coal, grain feed and all kinds of merchandise. The roundhouse was large enough to house the engine and two freight cars should they contain perishable goods or merchandise that would freeze in the winter. The engine always kept the house warm.

Along the line were cattle where the stock was loaded for the market; whole trainloads of sheep were shipped into Lake Fork valley for summer grazing. Also, the tie industry was the means of employment for many men, especially in the winter when things were slack. There were not many broad-gauge ties cut in this area as most of the tie timber was small. A tie was six feet in length, narrow gauge, with a minimum of six inches on the small end.

Anyone having timber could cut ties. They had to be piled or corded at the tracks so that an inspector could see through the pile and both ends of the tie. They were marked on the end of the ties with x, first class; o second class and the o, or ringers, were not paid for. Tie inspectors traveled all

Engine over the grade at Steele Draw.

over the system spotting ties. Each pile of ties had to have the name of the owner and his address. As the ties were spotted and tallied, the owners would be notifed of the number of first class, second class and ringers and would receive his pay. All the ringers which remained on the right of way for a period of thirty days became the property of the railroad company. These ties (ringers) were not paid for but were used by the company mostly on the switch or side tracks. In early days a first class tie of red spruce or pine brought 30 cents and the second class, mostly other woods, brought 25 cents. Later, as timbers became more scarce and wages increased, the railroad paid up to 49 cents and 44 cents for a narrow guage first class tie. There were many times that the ties had to be hauled from the rough or standing tree to the railroad track. If they were cut by hand, two experienced men could cut thirty to fifty ties a day, according to the timber, terrain and grouping of the timber. First the men would use a double hand crosscut saw to fall the trees. They worked together until they had a number of trees on the ground and then work separately to limb the tree, always leaving a few limbs on the underside of the tree to hold it upright and off the ground. Then, standing on the tree and using a double bit ax, they would score the sides of the entire tree that was to be used for ties. After scoring the bit ax was laid down for the old broad ax, and this is the one where the experienced man made the bark fly. Standing on the horizontal tree, the broad ax was swung over the head and the sides of the tree where it had been scored were taken off. This left the tree a perpendicular, almost smooth surface on the side of the log. Both sides of the log were thus hewn with the broad ax, the axman standing on and walking along the log, or tree, until both sides had been hewn, leaving a round surface on the top and bottom of the tree which would have to be peeled. The length of the tree worked would depend upon the number of ties that could be made from the stick which was measured by the ax handle marked by nitches cut on it measuring three feet. After the bark had been removed from the top of the log, the legs or limbs left on the side of the tree were cut and the bark removed. The ties all in one piece would not be cut in tie lengths unless they were to be packed out on burrows. Usually they were skidded by horse to the railroad and then cut into tie lengths before being piled for inspection.

The Lake City Pyretic Smelter located on the hillside adjoining the northeast corner of the townsite had been completed in 1909. Mr. Ramsey applied to the town for a right of way from the railroad track east of the Ocean Wave Mill for a spur to the smelter. This was granted. However, the spur was never built. The run of the regular train to and from Sapinero was three hours long. Sometimes a special train was sent into town. On one such occasion well remembered, Engineer Bob Grove came from Sapinero in two hours. The cattle on the ranches would stand on the track as it was dry and a good place to get warm. Bob never slowed up for the stock to get off the track. He only blew the whistle and went through them. At the Figure 5 ranch (now the VC) the train killed one cow and crippled four others. Some of them walked on three legs with the other leg hanging by the hide only. If these crippled animals were destroyed by the owners before the section foreman made his report the owners were not able to receive any damages from the railroad company, so the animals had to wander around until the foreman could be located. It was a very unpleasant sight! This ruling was made by the railroad company because some ranchers would place an old animal, horse, or cow, on the track so that they could claim the damages.

During the life of the Lake City Railroad, it was one of the best paying branches of the D&RG system. Howver, as the mines closed and other business-producing revenue for the road became less and less, the company applied to the PUC for abandonment in 1931. A hearing was held in the Court House at Lake City and the protest was so strong that abandonment at that time was not granted, pending increase in the revenue. But the increase did not come, and finally, in August, 1933, the branch was abandoned by the D&RG Company. Mr. Burke, owner of the Ute and Ule, bought the rails and right of way. Using a gas-powered automobile on the tracks, he operated this to and from Sapinero only a short time before the rails were purchased and removed by a junk company from Pueblo. Following the departure of the railroad came the improvement of highways into Lake City.

Southeast corner of kitchen showing under story completely carried away. Dick Halpin, night watchman, was in the kitchen when the slide struck. He was thrown completely out of the building, but was uninjured. Note sagging floor of upper story. Mrs. Watson, a cook, was asleep in this room, but escaped uninjured.

SNOWSLIDES

Snowslides claimed the lives of many miners in this area. The first of these, about which we have been able to learn, was the Dolly Varden slide in 1880, which killed three men. One was Henry C. Repath, who died trying to save two of his friends, both of whom were killed but whose names we did not learn. We found only a newspaper article which said of Mr. Repath, "a brave man, who gave his life trying to save two friends."

The next slide which took a life, we remember. It was in January 21st, 1916. A promising young man, Fred Davidson, with high hopes of a promising future, was caught in a slide at Nellie Gulch. Fred, in company with Harry Youmans and Otto Bowers, was coming down the gulch from Youmans saw mill when struck by the slide and carried to the bottom of the gulch. Bowers, who was partially covered, managed to get out and immediately started searching for his companions. In a few minutes he located Youmans and rescued him. Then the two started searching for Davidson, digging with all their might at the place where they calculated he might be. Finally, when nearly exhausted, they came upon the lifeless body, which had been buried ten feet deep by the avalanch. The team which they had been driving when struck by the slide was also killed.

The next slide to our knowledge was the worst. It was the Edna slide at the Empire Chief mine, which came down March 24, 1929, at 2:15 a.m. while everyone was in bed. The slide almost covered the two-story bunk house and boarding house. A one-story room at the end of the building was completely covered.

Dick Halpin, the night watchman, was in the kitchen when the slide struck, and was thrown completely out of the building, but was uninjured. The cook, Mrs. Mayme Watson, was asleep, but escaped uninjured. Jerald Strayer and J. Anderson were rescued after having been buried in eleven feet of snow for seven and eight hours. The victims killed by the slide were F. Wickersham, J. Color, Elmer Johnson and Keith Cutting. Of those caught in this slide two are still living— Jerald Strayer and Dick Halpin. A glass eye belonging to Jerald Strayer was found in the bedding.

The Independence slide which came down February 16, 1932, killed F. A. Walburg, who had started to walk to town from the mine. The weather and danger from other slides did not permit searching for Walburg's body before May, at which time a man named Foster was hired to look for the body. The story goes that Foster came upon the hand of Walburg the second day he started to work, but covered it up and continued to dig in order to earn more money. This went on for several days before he reported the body found.

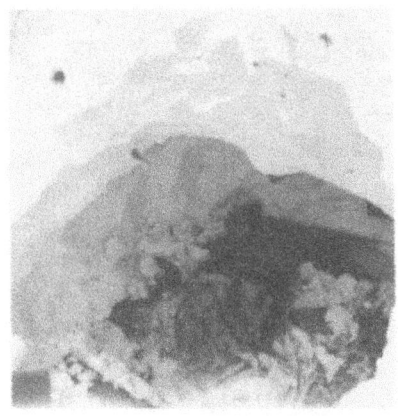

Recovering bodies of Cutting and Johnson. Note height of snow on end of two-story boarding house. Also opening to tunnel beneath about 12 feet of snow.

Holes from which bodies of Wickersham and Coler were recovered, and from which Strayer and Anderson were rescued after having been buried in 11 feet of snow for 7 and 8 hours respectively.

Hole from which body of Keith Cutting was recovered.

Rescuers standing in hole from which body of Elmer Johnson was removed.

Carrying out the body of Elmer Johnson after recovering it from the snow.

Bodies packed for the 15-mile sled trip to Lake City, Colorado.

LIBRARIES

There have been a number of libraries in Lake City, the first of which we have any knowledge was opened April, 1877, in the Seckles Building on Gunnison Avenue. There were other reading rooms opened during the years that lasted only a short time. The Baptist Church started a library sometime in the 90's and some of the books are still in the church. In 1901 Reverend Miln of the Baptist Church called for volunteers to help furnish a library, and a room in the Hough Building was donated for the purpose. Almost everyone in town donated books to this new project, and for a while many went there to read. But as mining declined and folks drifted away interest was lost and no one seems to know what became of the books.

The Federated Women's Club of Lake City started a library shortly after they organized in 1940 which they still maintain, although not much interest is shown in it at this time.

The Public School had a small library, but had very few books other than the Classics, a set of Encyclopedias, and a few books of fiction. After the advent of Reading Circle Books, the library was enlarged and new reference books were purchased by the school board. With the coming of Mr. and Mrs. Robert Sprout as teachers, the library took on a new significance and was built up considerably.

HINSDALE COUNTY SCHOOLS

As early as 1875 the early settlers realized that the greatest need was a school. Most of the residents believed that if they were to prosper here a free public school should be established. Several private schools had been started but not many could afford to pay for a private school. It was therefore decided to ask for the formation of a Lake City School District, money to be raised by subscription to be added to the small fund on hand. Accordingly, on January 3, 1876, a meeting was held and the following school board was elected: S. A. Dole, president; A. R. Thompson, secretary; and W. C. Lewman, treasurer.

The first school was started January 10 in a rambling wooden structure built almost on the street on upper Gunnison Avenue. It had four rooms downstairs and two upstairs which were used for lawyers' offices. The first teacher was W. A. McGinnis. His salary was fifty-five dollars a month. The first term, the money was raised by subscription, and a tax levied to take care of future terms. Tax collections were slow and by February of 1876 the school was in debt. The building used for the school was not satisfactory and people with children were beginning to leave. It was then decided to negotiate a bond issue for the purpose of building a school house.

At a public meeting June 15, 1880, the following resolution was adopted: "Resolved by the voters of this school meeting, held June 15th, 1880, in District One, Hinsdale County, that the Board of Directors thereof be directed to purchase the site selected by us this night and negotiate bonds at not less than ninety cents and proceed at once to let contracts for the erection of a schoolhouse on such plans and terms as may be thought best for the interest of this District." (*Silver World*, June 19, 1880)

Plans were drawn up accordingly by a Denver architect. Major Brockett was in charge of the school funds and was bonded accordingly. The plans called for a two-story stone building and a basement. There were to be two large rooms on the main floor and three rooms on the second—one large room and two smaller rooms. These specifications were not carried out, however, as the building is of brick, and there were two large rooms with a smaller room between on the second floor. The small room was used for a laboratory and a recitation room. Later it was also called the Principal's Office. Large cloakroom adjoined the outside rooms upstairs and down.

The October 16 issue of the *Silver World* published the following interesting information relative to the starting of work on the edifice. The cornerstone was laid October 9, 1880, the ceremonies being under the auspices of the local Masonic Lodge, Grand Master Herman Leuders directing the presentation of the program. After the ceremony of laying the cornerstone by the Grand Master and Grand Architect Wells, the following articles of historical and local significance were placed in a mortised receptacle of the stone within a tin box on which was printed the year of the masonry: a copy of Fossett's "Colorado" contributed by Henry C. Olney; *The Denver News, Tribune, Republican,* and *Post* of October 6, 1880; *New York World,* October 2, 1880; *Philadelphia Times,* October 2, 1880; *Silver World* first issue, June 19, 1875, and latest, October 9, 1880; *Lake City Mining Register,* October 8, 1880; *School Laws of Colorado;* roll of officers of school board, teachers and pupils; roll of county officers; roll of officers and members of Crystal Lake Lodge No. 34 A.F. & A.M.; specimens of ore from Ulay, Ocean Wave, Belle of the West, Edinburgh, Palmetto, Robertson, Silver Leaf and Silver Bonanza; a Spanish real by Henry C. Olney; old and new coins—German 1 pfennig, 2 pfennig and 10 pfennig, presented by Moritz Stockder; English penny, year 1863; Norwegian 1 ore, 1872, and Belgian 2 cent presented by W. S. Robertson; old Scotch penny, year 1707, presented by John Latimer; American coins—1 cent (1879), 5 cent (1854), 10 cent (1850), 25 cent (1864), and 50 cent (1859)—presented by Louis Weinberg; fractional currency; 10-cent piece presented by P. G. Dawson; views of Lake City, presented by Mrs. T. E. Barnhouse.

When the schoolhouse was remodeled in 1949 it was found necessary to remove the cornerstone because of a large crack down the wall. It was removed by workmen Saturday, April 23, in the presence of two members of the school board— H. T. Hoffman, secretary, and Mrs. William Wright, treasurer—the county superintendent, Mrs. Carolyn Wright, and a number of town folk. The tin box, which was enclosed in the receptacle of the stone, was removed and placed by the county

Lake City schoolhouse built in 1880. Picture taken in 1897 when Henry F. Lake was principal. Carolyn Hunt Wright third child from left; Clarence Wright boy on top right.

Schoolhouse as it looked in 1949 before remodeling.

clerk, Mrs. Mabel Rawson, in the vault at the Court House for safekeeping. Sunday the box was opened before a large crowd and found to contain the articles described above. When the stone was relaid later these additional items were placed with the original ones: a picture of Lake City, 1949; The Story of Lake City by Carolyn Wright; the roll of county and town officers and the school directors of District One; History of the First Presbyterian Church by John Adams; roll of school children and teacher; first issue of the *Lake City Tribune*, June 13, 1946; pictures of the county officials and school children with their teacher, Mrs. Edna Ramsey; Chamber of Commerce pamphlet of Lake City; *Gunnison News Champion* June 2, 1949; *Gunnison Courier* June 2, 1949; *Denver Post*; a number of coins contributed by the school children.

The *Silver World* of January, 1881, called attention of the school board to the lack of "terminal facilities" in connection with the new school, and two smaller buildings were erected back of the schoolhouse.

A small room off the high school room was built for a library, but a set of the classics, an old set of encyclopedias, and the *Book of Knowledge*. Miss Mabel Burnett, head of the *Americana* and *Book of Knowledge*, and a friend of mine, gave us a new set of reference books when I ordered the other books. By 1959 we had the beginning of a fairly good library. When Mr. and Mrs. Robert Sprout were hired to teach in 1960 they had new library shelves placed in the big hall and built up a remarkable library for such a small school. Mrs. Sprout had had library training and a great deal of credit is due her for her extra work in this line.

Going back to the first school district—as the population grew, more districts were formed in the county until there were eight districts. One, of course, remained at Lake City. District Two was later organized at Capitol City; Three, at Lake Shore; Four, at Henson; Five, at Cathedral; Seven, at Hermit, and Eight, at Debs. Later, as the population dwindled, the smaller districts were absorbed by One. District Eight, at Debs, became a joint district with Archuletta County, known as Joint 50. In 1960 Districts One and Five consolidated, making District One a first class district and called Hinsdale County School 1.

The schoolhouse at Capitol City, built in 1883, was a very large white frame building, and has been torn down. I taught two terms of school there. It was a summer school, because the winters were too severe to hold school there in that season. The schoolhouse at Lake Shore burned down several years ago after it had been sold for a summer home. The

Schoolhouse after it was remodeled in 1949. The lady in the picture is Bessie Kirk, who started to school here in the 90's.

Capitol City schoolhouse built in 1883. Was still in good condition when torn down a few years ago for lumber.

schoolhouse at Henson, a beautiful small log building, was dismantled some years ago. The schools at Hermit and Debs were held in private houses.

There were five teachers until 1941 when the staff was cut to three. H. G. Heath was principal and taught the high school grades, Carolyn Wright taught the grammar and intermediate grades and Mrs. Edna Ramsey had the primary. It was later cut to two teachers and Mr. Heath and Mrs. Ramsey taught the first eight grades. While the old school building was being repaired, Mrs. Ramsey held school at the Swank Apartments. Mrs. Wright taught one high school pupil that year and the following year taught one eighth-grader, one ninth-grader and one twelfth-grader in her home. School was held the following year in the remodeled schoolhouse with two teachers carrying the load of grades one through twelve until 1959 when again three teachers were hired. By 1963 the school population had again dropped and two teachers were hired for that year. High school pupils had by this time started entering in Gunnison or Montrose in order to graduate from an accredited school and participate in athletics.

The first annual high school commencement was held in the Armory Hall in May, 1898, for those finishing the tenth grade. The graduates were Burnie Patterson, Lulu and Mary Lawler, Edith Bent, Alice Donnell, Sadie Isaacs and Ray Madison. Henry F. Lake was the principal. He later became owner and editor of the *Gunnison News Champion.* Forty-eight years from that date the last commencement was held in the Armory, with only one graduate—Lillian Bernice Rawson. The principal that year was Carolyn Wright. Many have graduated since that year, but after the schoolhouse was remodeled programs were held in the school auditorium.

The first twelfth-grade graduation held in the Armory hall was on May 3, 1901. The principal was H. G. Hoff and the assistant was H. G. Heath, who later became principal. The graduates were Valeria Patterson and Rene B. Wright. The first baccalaureate sermon was preached in the Presbyterian Church by Reverend J. W. Todd. The names of those taking part in this program will be of interest to the readers. Following is the program as taken from the invitation in the possession of Rene B. Wright.

Violin Solo------------------------------------C. L. Sweet

Invocation--------------------------------Rev. M. B. Milne

Song-------------------------------------Primary Room

Solo----"Hush, My Little One"--------Mrs. George Denise

Oration----"Myths"--------------------Valeria Patterson

Song---------------------------------------Male Quartet

Calisthenic Drill----------------------------------Primary

Song----"Golden Boat"----------------------Intermediate

Oration----("_____")---------------------Rene Wright

Violin Solo------------------------------------C. L. Sweet

Solo----"That Melody Divine"------------------Mrs. Uglo

Maypole Drill----Grammar Grade Pupils (I was in that drill)

Presentation of Diplomas and
    Class Address-----------President George Richards

Violin Solo--Mr. Sweet

Benediction--------------------------Reverend J. W. Todd

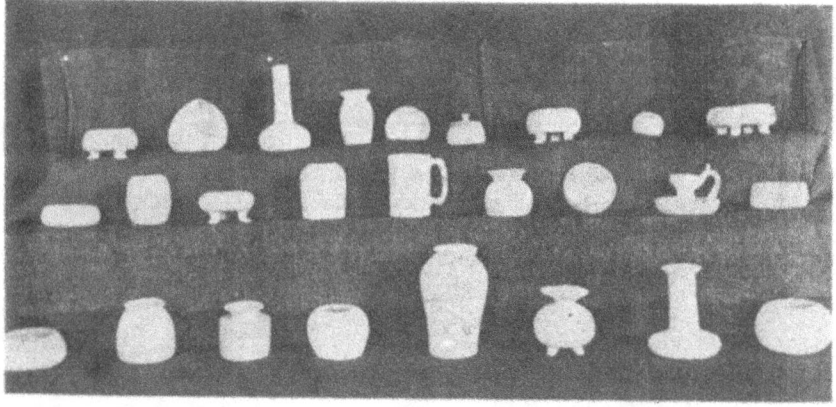

Clay modeling done by the Lake City High School with clay from the Slumgullion slide.

THE FIRST PRESBYTERIAN CHURCH OF LAKE CITY AND OTHER CHURCHES

Acting under the authority of the Presbytery of Colorado, the Reverend Alex M. Darley, Missionary Pastor of San Juan County, visited Lake City, Hinsdale County, Colorado. Arriving on June 15, 1876, he spent that day and the two days following visiting every house and tent in Lake City, up the Lake Fork of the Gunnison three miles and down the Lake Fork six miles. As a result of this visit he secured ten names to a petition to the Presbytery of Colorado for the organization of a church at Lake City, Colorado.

After the meeting Sunday morning, June 28, 1876, in Brockett's Hall, five more persons added their names to the list, making twenty-five charter members. (Of these twenty-five persons, there were six different denominations represented.) They were Mr. C. H. Sweetser, Mrs. Sarah E. Taft, Mrs. Agnes P. Gormer, Mrs. R. W. Jordan, Mrs. J. M. Dennis, Mrs. Eliza Nye, Mrs. Emma Hughes, David Anderson, Mrs. Sarah P. Bartolf, Mrs. Margaret Wood, Washington L. Brasler, Shepard G. Patrick, Jr., David McConnell, Solomon Erickson, and Allen T. Gunnell.

At noon, after prayer, the Reverend Darley (Elder Stanley Larson of Del Norte was appointed as clerk of the meeting), C. H. Sweetser, David McConnell, and Shepard G. Patrick, Jr., were chosen as elders.

Allen T. Gunnell, Solomon Erickson, and Washington L. Brasler were chosen as deacons. These persons, accepting the confession of faith, and the Government of the Presbyterian Church of these United States of America, were duly declared an organized church, The First Presbyterian Church of Lake City, Hinsdale County, Colorado. This was the first church organization of any kind in Lake City, and as far as is known, on the Western Slope in the State of Colorado.

At the evening service at eight p.m., these chosen officers were ordained and installed into their respective offices. The services of the day were well attended, being between 100 and 150 present. That evening the first church choir was

Two views of the Presbyterian Church, first church on the Western Slope of Colorado, dedicated November 29, 1876.

Episcopal Church, built in December, 1876.

heard in Lake City; also the first church offering was taken. There was much interest manifested during the day, not only regarding the organization, but also in the building of a church edifice in Lake City.

On June 20, Reverend Darley started solicitations for funds toward the erection of a church building in Lake City and in two days received cash and pledges to the account of $518.75. At the first prayer meeting, held in Lake City that night, June 21, the trustees were ordered to purchase two lots at the corner of Fifth Street and Gunnison Avenue for the purpose of building a church and a manse. At this meeting there was also a bible school organized, which was to meet in Truner's carpenter shop each Lord's day.

When the church building was dedicated, November 29, 1876, the membership was 23. Although there has never been any official record written in the minutes, we have, through study of the records and membership register, come to the information that the highest membership was in 1889. At that time the membership was around 130. The only official record in the minutes is in April, 1922; the membership was at that time 32.

As to the building of the manse, there is no record, with this exception: November 18, 1876, the session met in the "Pastorage."

From the book *Pioneering in the San Juan* by the first pastor, we find that the bell was bought and paid for by one Theodore S. Little, Sr., of Morristown, New Jersey. He also paid the freight on the bell, which amounted to more than the first cost, as it was hauled across the Continental Divide and two mountain ranges—the Sangre de Cristo and the Sierra Madre—all the way from Pueblo by team and wagon. The bell that made this trip was taken from the steeple and replaced in 1882 or 1883, but we cannot find what then happened to the first bell.

The following have pastored this church: Alex M. Darley, George M. Darley, H. M. Whaling, Charles Fueller, J. R. Cooper, Joseph Gaston, J. R. Lamb, J. W. Todd, W. A. White, William Eadie, and others of whom there is no record.

The church was without a pastor for a number of years although the members tried to keep the Sunday School going. In June, 1947, a missionary minister, John Adams, came to Lake City and held services until January, 1955. Since that time the church has been served by student ministers during the summer months and services carried on during the winter months by lay members, with an occasional visit from ministers of other churches and of the different moderators. Rev. Howard Manning, John Adams, Rev. Philip Ramer of Ouray, Rev. Stanton of Delta, and Rev. Knox of Montrose were some of the moderators. Student ministers have been: Delbert Wimple, Gordon Ingram, Tom Wilbanks, James Harder, Don Shoemaker, and Gordon Bechtel.

According to the *Silver World* of December 9, 1876, the second church established in Lake City was the Episcopal. The paper announced the meeting to be held on December 11 and by the following January regular services were scheduled. Regular services continued until May, 1880, without a regular pastor, when the Reverend A. D. Drummand, the first pastor, was called to the church. The Easter service in 1881 drew a good crowd and was described by the *Silver World* in a glowkng manner. Shortly after that Reverend Drummand was called to Gunnison and the church was again without a pastor, although Sunday School was continued. The church was incorporated August 5, 1893 under the name The St. James Mission Parish Church. Services continued with lay members in charge, with an occasional resident minister. The church building was much smaller than the Presbyterian Church, but held a dignified position in the community. It still stands across the street from the Presbyterian Church and is kept in good repair. Services are held occasionally in the summer months.

The first Methodist Church services were held in the Presbyterian church every other Sunday until the Presbyterians needed their building each. The Methodists then started holding services in the schoolhouse. Later they met at the Court House, but the congregation dwindled until 1878 when the church lots were sold to Colonel Charles McDougall, and the Methodists worshipped with those of other faiths.

The first Baptist revival was held March 8, 1885, at the end of which eighteen members joined those who in September, 1883, had decided to organize a Baptist church. The charter members were: Mrs. Jennie Bent, Mrs. J. J. Frank, Mr. and Mrs. J. M. Talliferro, Mr. and Mrs. F. M. Mendenhall, Mrs. A. Johnson, Mr. and Mrs. J. L. Murphy, C. Thompson, Mr. and Mrs. P. P. Kennedy, Mr. and Mrs. J. S. Hough, Mrs. E. Fluallen, Mrs. George Ferguson, Mr. and Mrs. W. I. Edgerton. The following officers were elected: Deacons, F.M. Mendenhall and J.B. Talliferro; Clerk, Mrs. J.S. Hough; Treasurer, J. L. Murphy; and Trustees, P. P. Kennedy, C. Thompson, J. S. Hough, C. E. Bent, and W. I. Edgerton.

The first baptisms were made at Third Street in a large tank which was filled from the creek. Rev. M. A. Clark officiated while the congregation sang hymns.

Lots on Bluff Street were purchased in January of 1890 and the foundation for the church was laid in April 1891. The building was completed that year. It had one large room and

Baptist Church, built in 1891. Shown in the Sunday School, 1925. House in left background, home of John S. Hough, once a candidate for governor of Colorado. Mr. Hough stands with cane in front of his home. Right background, the parsonage.

The Catholic Church of St. Rose of Lima, built in 1881.

a smaller Sunday School room. It is the only church in Lake City that boasts of beautiful leaded glass windows, memorials to some of its first members.

The first services in the church were held September 20, with Reverend C. A. Parker in charge. The building was dedicated January 17, 1892, with Reverend Alex Turnbell preaching the morning service and Reverend D. H. Woods the evening service. Reverend D. E. McGlashan was the minister from 1894 to 1897. He was very strict about the behavior of the members, and at one time called a meeting of the members to examine those taking part in worldly amusements, especially dancing, card playing, drinking, etc. A later minister, in 1909, threatened to expel members for dancing.

The religious influence of all the churches had a lasting effect on those that followed.

In September, 1877, a priest, Father Hayes, from Del Norte, came to Lake City to raise funds for a Catholic church. He conducted high mass in the Court House and while here raised $800.

The building was dedicated January 6, 1878, although it was not completed until March of that year. It was named Catholic Church of St. Rose of Lima. The *Silver World* of October 29, 1881, described the church as a "frame building 22 x 55 feet. The ceiling is arched, providing fine acoustics. Wainscoting 3-1/2 feet high of grained oak with walnut trim runs around the sanctuary walls. The painting is to be done by a professional artist. The altar will be of marble and highly ornamented. An addition 14 x 21-1/2 feet is being placed on the rear of the building. It will be partitioned into two rooms and used by the priest."

Father J. H. Brunker conducted services there February, 1882. Father Quinn of Gunnison Catholic Church conducted services from time to time. Other visiting priests made frequent trips to Lake City for mass. One that we remember quite well was Father Kipp, who performed a number of Catholic weddings here. One couple that he married, Sadie Mallon and William McCarley, and who later moved to Denver, were happy to have him at their golden wedding which they celebrated a number of years ago in Denver. He also married Joseph White and Mary Doran, early Lake City residents.

Three years ago a number of enterprising Catholics decided they should do something for the upkeep of the church. The building was redecorated inside and out. Originally painted white, it was painted a beautiful shade of rose. The addition on the back used for the priests, which had been torn away, was replaced by a new one, and flowers were planted in the yard. Built on a hill, it can be admired from far down the street.

FIRES AND EARLY BUILDINGS

Prior to 1880 all of the buildings in town were frame and built very close together; when a fire broke out all of the surrounding buildings were endangered. The first major fire was the south half of block 55, where the Hough Block now stands. This fire destroyed all of the buildings to the old Pueblo House. There was not enough fire equipment or water supply to stop the fire. Another large fire destroyed the buildings along Silver Street from the *Silver World* office on Fourth and Silver to the last building on the corner of Third and Silver. This fire burned the Hank Richart livery barn, a two-story store building, the law office of H. A. Avery, and Gunst clothing store.

A fire also destroyed the Old Occidental Hotel located on Silver Street almost opposite the Pueblo House. At the time this hotel was operated by D. T. McLeod. H. A. Avery later built the cement building where the Lake City Drug Store stands. Charles Watsom established his shoe store across the street in the building which is now the Sports Shop, located just south of the Carey Building.

Block #58, located between Second and Third Streets and Silver and Gunnison Avenue, was burned by two fires. The buildings on Third Street were built solidly together from Silver Street to Gunnison Avenue with the only open space being the alley. The buildings burned on this street were the two-story LaVeta Hotel, on the corner of Third and Gunnison Avenue; the Whitmore Building, from the hotel to the alley; from the alley to Silver Street, the restaurant, Dolan Confectionery, and the Corner Saloon. Also burned on Silver Street were the buildings between Third and Second, which included the Corner Saloon, Barbershop, Senate Saloon, Al (Gummys) Forrest's Candy Store and Soda Fountain, Carey Saloon, Penniston's General Merchandising, Maurer's Jewelry, and the former City Hall and Fire House. The only dwellings left on this block were the Doctor Rapp house, the Dinsmore house, and the building of the first school on Second and Gunnison Avenue.

Another fire was 'at the Crystal Palace on Bluff Street between Second and Third. This was the largest house in the red light district. The fire occurred in the middle of the night and there was no chance of putting it out. The night was still and clear and full-sized red shingles could be seen in the sky red-hot as the heat from the fire popped them into the air.

There were two livery stables which were located almost on the same lot which were destroyed in two separate fires. The stables were on the east side of Silver Street between First and Second just north of Henson Creek. The first stable to burn was that of Emos Slough. It burned all of the buildings and feed. The Hider stable was next. He built his buildings on the same lot as the previous fire. The Hider fire occurred about dusk and destroyed everything, including seven horses. All of these horses except one were taken from the stables and turned loose, but the fright caused them to run down Silver Street and right back into the burning stables, where they burned to death. They could be seen lying on their backs and their cries were heard all over town. A horse cannot be led out of a fire except by blindfolding him and leading him to safety and then tying him fast to prevent his returning to his home.

Another tragic fire was at the old log jail built in 1876. This building was located on the east side of Third and Henson Street. Kit Carter, who had had too much liquor, was placed in the jail after he had given a gun to Steve Kinsey in in the county jail. Carter must have been smoking, but the actual cause of the fire was never determined. The charred body was found in the smouldering ruins.

The entrance to Henson Creek Canyon was the site of another tragic fire. A baby girl was burned to death in the house. The fire was extinguished but too late to save the baby's life.

The county jail building was completely destroyed by fire, but fortunately there were no inmates at the time of the fire. Sheriff Coburn escaped by jumping from the upper story window. Only the steel cells remained after this fire.

The last major fire was at the last Occidental Hotel, situated on the north end of Block #55, just across the street from the Silver World office. Only a part of the Pueblo House remains today. This is the location of the Forbes Antique Shop; the upper story and south wing have been removed. At the time of the fire which burned Hank Richard's livery stable, all the buildings on the east side of Silver Street were protected by hanging bedding on ropes from the tops of the buildings and keeping this bedding wet with the hose. However, all the fronts of these buildings had to be repainted.

No major fires occurred in the Bank block, #57, and five of the original business houses built in the early 70's are still in use. These buildings are: Zeno Felder's Drugstore, Goodwin Laundry Building, Kafka Clothing, P. P. Kennedy Dry Goods and the building, once the post office, now the Women's Club Building.

There are also some log buildings remaining which were built prior to 1880. A house on the east side of Gunnison Avenue between Fourth Street and Second has been covered with siding and the logs are not visible. An old log cabin stands on the alley of Forberg's lots between Fourth and Fifth Streets. The kitchen of the Jack Vicker's home is now sided over. But it was formerly one of the old log houses; also the former Adshade residence, located on the east side of Gunnison Avenue between Fifth and Sixth Streets.

The house on lot #30 on the east side of Silver Street between Sixth and Seventh Streeets was the site of the home of the old Negro slave and his wife, Willis Williams. The logs are not visible at present as they have been sided over, as is the main part of the Tom Ray residence in West Lake, west side of Bluff Street between Seventh and Eighth Streets, now the home of Mrs. Mendenhall.

Another old log building of the early days was the one standing on the corner of Fifth and Silver on the southeast corner. This cabin is still standing as it was built and the logs are not covered. Another old log building was the Hunter cabin on the southwest corner of Fifth and Silver Streets. This building has been sided over. Next to it on the north is the log cabin of F. M. Mendenhall, built in 1879, which has also been sided over and is presently occupied by the grandson, Frank Mendenhall.

Mr. and Mrs. James Wells live in the well preserved log house owned by her grandparents, the A. McLauchlins.

Fire that destroyed Hank Richart's barn and other buildings. Building on extreme left was once Lake City post office. Note board walk.

The first Hough Volunteer Fire Company. No. 2—Lucius Talliferro, cousin of Mrs. Ruth Edgerton Stephenson. No. 7—Mrs. Stephensen's father. No. 11—W. S. Whinnery, the only one still living.

FIRE FIGHTING

In 1877 the Town decided that some kind of protection against fires should be provided. It was at this time that the ditches were dug from Henson Creek through the main streets of the town. These ditches are still in use. Prior to the ditches there were wells dug at intersections of streets for fire protection. In 1878 the town purchased a Babcock hand pump and hose so that the wells could be utilized to fight fires. At this time a hook and ladder cart was also purchased by the Town. The hook was a twenty-foot pipe with handles along one end and a chain at the other. At the same end with the chain was a hook that could be used to reach into the fire to pull down a burning wall. There were three twenty-five-foot ladders built so that they could be extended as one ladder.

The hook and ladder wagon was longer than the ordinary cart, with a short tongue. A rope was tied to the tongue so that additional men could help pull the cart. Along the sides of the cart were leather buckets with handles for a bucket brigade. This car is lying in the street at the City Hall and soon will be only a remembrance. One of the ladders is stored in the barn at the San Juan Ranch.

Before 1893 the Hough Fire Company was known as such, but it was not until that year that the Hough Fire Company #1 was recorded with the Secretary of State, with the following charter members: H. P. Lyons, J. F. Steinbeck, W. I. Edgerton, S. S. Eddy, W. S. Whinnery, and Ed Rowan. There were now two hose carts and the hook and ladder wagon. The equipment was moved from Gunnison Avenue to lot #19 of block 58 in 1909.

The fire bell remained on the lot owned by Mrs. Lizzie Karl across the alley from the Court House and in 1901 the Town paid Mrs. Karl $18 rental for the ground on which the old wooden belfry stood. The bell remained at this location until 1911 when the Town donated $25 to the firemen to purchase a new steel tower, which was moved with the fire equipment to the new location at Second and Silver Street. A new chemical engine was purchased by the town consisting of a cart and two tanks for chemicals to create pressure for the fire hoses from the engine. While one tank was being used the other tank could be charged. The first fire on which the new chemical was used was on the corner of Sixth and Silver Street, where the Wrights now live. A huge pile of wooden boxes were saturated with kerosene and set on fire. The fire bell was rung and the chemical engine drawn by eight fleet-footed men was rushed to the fire and it was extinguished immediately.

The Hough Fire Company served as a volunteer fire department until it became inactive in 1940. This chemical engine can now be seen in the Town Hall.

The fire house and equipment was later moved from 2nd and Silver Street to the present location on Third and Bluff Streets. The steel cells for the jail were also moved to this new location.

In 1950 the County leased a part of the City Hall where county jail cells were installed with adjoining living quarters for the sheriff. In 1962 the County surrendered their lease to the Town and now the entire building and equipment belongs to the City and the County has the use of the jail when necessary.

A closer view of the Baptist Church, shown also on page 73.

ELECTRICITY

Before electricity there were other means of lighting in the homes and stores. Tallow candles were the first to be used. They were made in tin candle molds, either single or several molds fastened together. A wick string was inserted in the mold and kept in the center of the mold by syspension. The tallow was heated and poured into the mold and allowed to cool. Then the mold was immersed in hot water long enough for the tallow to slip out of the mold and another fill made. Kerosene was also used but it had to be shipped by freight so that it was not always available away from the town. I had an inventory from the Schiffer store in Lake City that showed the purchase of one gallon of kerosene for $1.50 and on the same invoice was one gallon of whiskey at $.75.

In 1880 electricity was generated in Lake City by George W. Crowe at the Ocean Wave Mill at the north end of Henson Street between Eighth and Ninth. Steam was used for power and later a water turbine replaced the steam plant at the same location. At the same time there was also another steam plant at the old stone building on Fourth and Henson. The latter plant furnished the street lights for the town while Crowe's plant furnished the street lights for the town's residences. The homes were lighted by carbon bulb. The arc lamps were used on the streets and had to be adjusted each day for use at night. The plants were run at night as there was no use for the juice during the day. All of the early wiring was done with porcelain knobs, tubes and cleats. This type of wiring was safe and lasted when properly installed. Some of the wiring in the old houses is still in use. While this old wire is too small to carry the load now used for modern purposes, it was ample for lighting only. Each tap for an outlet from the run was not only well taped over soldered joints, but each outlet for a light at the rosette. A lead fuse was also used so that overloaded, this fuse would blow and the remainder of the circuit would not be affected. When the schoolhouse was remodeled in 1950, soldered joints with the knob and tube construction was still in use.

In 1902 a franchise was given the Hinsdale Mining and Development Company for lights in the town and water was used in the plant at the Granite Fall, south of town. From 1910-1913 the electric power line was extended to the Pelican Mine two miles up Henson Creek where a compressor was run with an electric motor. This company operated until 1933 when the dam was washed out and the light plant was abandoned. The town was without lights until 1939 when Mr. Schallar operated a small plant with a gas motor, which supplied only a part of the town with juice. For a number of years the business houses and some of the residences installed their own light plants. George Fessor obtained franchise to supply the town with lights, purchasing juice from the Valley View Ranch. This was not sufficient power to supply the town so he purchased a diesel engine to run the generator. This plant was used until he moved the plant to Granite Falls near the old site to obtain electric power. He operated this plant until 1957 when he sold his franchise to the REA, who brought lines in from Gunnison by way of Powderhorn and up the Lake Fork. The REA extended their line up the Lake Fork to cottages at the Lake and Castle Lakes located just north of Child's Park.

Another view of the Empire Chief snow slide of March 24, 1929—rescuers starting work on the trench from which bodies were recovered.

TELEPHONE

In 1881 telephone service was put into use from Lake City to Capitol City, Rose's Cabin, Ouray, Mineral Point, Animas Forks and Silverton. The line lasted until 1893.

The first telegraph service was installed by D. W. Bouton for Western Union in 1876 and the first message was to the governor of the State. This service lasted until the railroad came in 1889. Then the telegraph service of the railroad was used until the granting of franchise to Western Union in 1902, when messenger service was also provided in the town.

The source of power for the first telegraph was from the old type of Crows Foot Batteries, in gallon glass jars with carbon and lead cells in acid. The office was in the house on Bluff Street between Third and Fourth Streets, which was later purchased by H. E. Wright. Many of the glass jars were left there and were later used for canning of wild strawberry cold pack and jellies of currants and gooseberries which Clarence and Carolyn Wright picked at White Cross in 1911.

A franchise was granted W. C. Blair in 1906 for telephone service in Lake City. The service was to be in operation by August, 1907, or the franchise would be withdrawn. The service was not established.

The Colorado Telephone Company was granted a franchise for telephone service in the town in 1909. This company extended their line to the Frank Hough and Wyoming mines on upper Henson. Later the Mountain States Telephone Company took over the lines and installed toll lines to Ouray and Gunnison. As business decreased there was not enough use for these lines and the Mountain States abandoned their toll lines and the local service came from switchboard in Lake City. The Hinsdale County Telephone Company was given a franchise in 1950 and in 1961 dial service was installed.

Col. C. F. Meek, operating the Carson district, built a telephone line from Lake City to Carson, and also up the Lake Fork over Cinnamon Pass to Animas Forks and Silverton. Mr. Meek also operated the Lyon Tunnel below Animas Forks.

He surveyed a proposed railroad through the range from the Lyton Tunnel to the White Cross Valley. The portal of this tunnel, which was about 50 feet in length, was large enough for the narrow-gauge train. The Meek telephone line was a private line extending from Lake City to Carson, Animas Forks and Silverton.

Carolyn and Clarence Wright, authors of this volume, on their fiftieth anniversary.

WATER WORKS BONDS

In the year 1889 twenty-five $1,000 bonds were issued at 8% interest per annum. A special election held in 1905 for voting on refunding the water works bonds was declared irregular and another election was necessary. On February 15, 1906, another special election was held for the purpose of refunding the water works bonds. As a result of this election 48 bonds of $500 each were to be issued at the rate of 6% interest per annum. This total amounted to $24,000 and only one bond had been taken up since the first issue.

Again in 1924, water works bonds were refunded in the amount of $23,000 at 6% interest per annum. This total amounted to $24,000 and only one bond had been taken up since 1906. August of 1949 saw the last $500 water works bond paid. This bond drew interest in the amount of $2,000, so that it cost $2,500 to retire it. The following table illustrates the entire cost of retiring the water works bonds:

```
8% interest on $25,000 for 17 years............$34,000
6% interest on $24,000 for 18 years............ 25,000
6% interest on the balance until paid...........  6,000

     Interest paid......................$65,000
     Original bonds ....................  25,000
     Total cost of bonds ................$90,000
```

(Table from Minutes of the Town of Lake City 1889-1949.)

There was no attempt to retire one or two bonds each year and the amount spent for interest could have retired the bonds in about twenty years.

The Lake City water works system consisted of a log dam above the Granite Falls, cast-iron 8-inch pipe from the dam to Third and Gunnison where the line was reduced to 6-inch spiral steel pipe and continued north on Gunnison Avenue to Seventh Street. Also at the point of Third and Gunnison a 6-inch line was extended west on Second Street to Silver Street and north on Silver Street to Seventh Street. A 6-inch line was extended west on Third Street to Bluff Street. There were 13 fire plugs located on the southwest corners of the street intersections.

The rental for use during the summer was not sufficient to keep up the needed repairs although during the first twenty years there was very little spent for this purpose. For many years there was a frontage tax levied on property for water works; however, this tax was later declared illegal and was no longer collected. In 1926 the Ladies Union Aid contributed to the Town in cash the sum of $363.75 for purchase of pipe for the water works. In 1933, however, the dam washed out and the water system was abandoned.

Fourth of July celebration, 1897. Drilling contest.

EARLY-DAY ENTERTAINMENT AND RECREATION

In the 70's, a number of large halls were erected for entertainment. One of these was Kelly's—a beautiful building with a main hall and a shooting gallery. This building, according to the *Silver World* of April 8, 1877, opened in April. Here they had dancing, target shooting, and a bar. Brocketts Hall was also built in 1877, and was used for all sorts of entertainment. Here a ball was given to raise money for a band. There were several billiard halls, the first of which was probably that of Frank Esensperber. It also had a saloon and a club room for cards.

In June of 1878 Fred Hilgenhaus, well remembered by the Wrights, opened the Lake City Beer Gardens up Henson Creek. It was a beautiful spot in a natural setting, made more attractive by artistic placement of tables and chairs, rustic walks among the willows which grew there, benches, arbors and swings. A large platform was built for dancing with music furnished by the management. The area was later ruined by a flood coming down Henson Creek.

By July 1877 there were about thirty saloons operating in and on the outskirts of Lake City. Some were classed as "respectable" places of amusement, while others were known as the honky-tonk variety. We have not been able to see much difference, other than that of the people who frequented them. A man could get just as drunk in one as the other as long as he had money to spend. We once saw a man thrown out of one of the so-called "respectable" places and kicked in the face after he landed in the ditch. He had been welcome when he first cashed his check. Of course, LADIES did not drink in those days.

Most national holidays were celebrated in a big way from earliest days in Lake City. The churches had Christmas programs as did the schools, and always had beautifully decorated Christmas trees with gifts for the children. The trees were lighted with colored candles. There was always a

Santa Claus to pass out the candy and toys. I remember one program at the Baptist church. The committee had arranged for a Santa and when he appeared, the minister, Joel Wood, stopped the program. He did not believe in telling the children about Santa Claus. A vote was taken and the Santa proceeded with his part of the program. The minister's little girl, aged five, was only allowed to receive a pair of black mittens and a Bible, and was told that there was no Santa Claus.

We no longer have Christmas programs in all the churches, but celebrate Christmas as a community in the Presbyterian Church, where everyone is welcome to hear again the story of Christ's birth and the children are given candy and fruit. No child is left out. The members of the Union Ladies Aid Society fill the candy sacks which are passed out by Santa Claus.

The Fourth of July always calls for a big celebration. The first Independence Day celebration on the Western Slope was held in Lake City in 1875. The first flag was flown that day over the office of the *Silver World*. It was made of red flannel drawers, a blue flannel shirt and a large white handkerchief.

The day was celebrated with races and contests of different kinds. One contest of great interest was the drilling contest, which we still have. A large hard rock is placed on a platform and different teams compete to see who can drill the deepest hole in the shortest time.

A public dance in the Armory ended the celebration which usually began at nine o'clock and often lasted until daylight. A supper was served at midnight, sometimes in the hall by some organization for the purpose of raising money.

From the earliest days fireworks played a large part in the Fourth of July celebrations. Firecrackers could be heard all through the day, with large displays at night put on by the various stores and organizations. Folks were usually awakened at daybreak by a large blast of powder set off in the hills nearby.

When the Wrights were in business they put on an annual display which could be seen for miles on the big penninsula at the Lake San Cristobal.

It is impossible to describe here all the celebrations of the early years, but one in 1884, as described in the Lake City *Mining Register* of July 11, 1884, is certainly worth mentioning.

The parade was led by the Pitkin Guards in full uniform, followed by the Drum Corp, The Hough Fire Company, the members carrying flags with the letters J. S. H. E. Co. No. 1, and the hook and ladder truck drawn by six horses; a float

Close-up of drilling contest.

Pioneer Jubilee Club Room—before and after. This was one of the oldest and most run-down buildings in town. President of the club at the time, Mrs. Ellen Zeigler Wells, granddaughter of the pioneer A. McLauchlin, took it over for the club project of the year and the picture shows the results. The inside of the building was also beautifully remodeled and book shelves built to house the library, another project of the club.

carrying thirty-eight ladies dressed in white and each carrying a state flag representing the thirty-eight states; and a group of men and women on horseback from the Ulay mine. At the ceremony following the parade flags were arranged as a background, with the thirty-eight ladies representing the states arranged in a semi-circle. At 3 p.m. the mayor, the Honorable J. C. Bell called the assembly to order and the Reverend Charles Fuller opened the program with a prayer followed by music "Hail Natal Day," composed by local men, George Wilson and Carl Patz. This was followed by speeches by M. B. Gerry, Col. Van Eps, C. C. Wattles, and B. B. Galvin, with appropriate songs between speeches.

Memorial Day celebrations were started on May 30, 1883. There was a parade starting at Third Street and Gunnison Avenue at 2 p.m. and ending at the I.O.O.F. Cemetery. Members of the G.A.R., Pitkin Guards, Hough Fire Co., and I.O.O.F. Lodge followed by men on horseback led the parade. These were followed by carriages with men, women and children; although many came on foot.

Services were held at the grave of the murdered Sheriff Campbell by the G.A.R. and I.O.O.F. The speaker was G. W. Henry, assisted by the Reverend Charles Fuller, who pronounced the benediction. All the soldiers' graves were decorated with American flags and the I.O.O.F. graves with lodge flags.

From that day on there was always a parade and speeches on Memorial Day up until about twenty years ago when the population had dwindled and most of those who had promoted the ceremonies were among the dead. The later parades were led by the bands for many years. Prominent in the parades for many years were the veterans of the Civil War. George Rawlings, who had played the fife and the drum in the War, marched proudly in the parades as did my uncle, J. A. Hunt, W. I. Edgerton and others. We still have the drumsticks that my father, W. P. Hunt, used. He taught our son William to keep time with them on the bottom of a chair when he was only two years old. William later played drums in an orchestra.

Washington's Birthday was also celebrated with a parade, with all the school children, flags in hand, taking part. Some of these are described in the article about "Nigger" Willis in another part of the book.

Later the Firemen's Masquerade Ball became an annual affair and continued until about 1935. Invitations were issued and had to be shown behind closed curtains when the masks were raised for identification. This was done to prevent the lawless element from Hell's Acres from attending. The best music available was always furnished at these balls.

Lake City was luckier in the earlier days than now to be on the circuit of the traveling shows and circuses. Then the shows came in overland and were shown in large tents. After the railroad was built they came in by train but were still shown in tents.

On one occasion the folks got some extra laughs free. The circus cars were sidetracked on the siding between Second and Sixth Streets, and unloaded the animals. There was a wooden bridge there which the elephants refused to cross, so the trainers had to ford the river with them. There was a deep hole below the bridge and when the elephants got there they refused to come out. They began to shower each other with water and were having a wonderful time when they spotted the crowd on the bridge watching them and proceeded to drench them with water. The trainers had to get in the water with them and goad them out of the water. There was a Dog and Pony Show that made Lake City for many years and no better trained animals have we ever seen. It was a great disappointment to those of us left in Lake City when the population no longer paid the owners to come our way. We can remember when stage plays, such as East Lynn and Uncle Tom's Cabin, were shown here in tents. The last one I remember was in 1905.

Many road companies came to Lake City after the Opera House, later simply known as the Armory, was built. Magicians were very popular about that time. There are still folks here who remember the time a magician of some note performed in the Armory. There was a crowd of young men in the audience who claimed they could not be hypnotized. The magician proceeded to hypnotize them from the stage, and throwing a make-believe rope, told them they were lassoed and brought them, pulling back like cattle, up to the stage. He then pointed to the side of the stage and told the boys it was a swimming pool and for them to take a swim. After they started to disrobe he awakened them, but the young man who had laughed the loudest was down to his underwear and had started to take it off when he was snapped out of it. The crowd went wild.

In 1876 the first dramatic club was organized and the play "Among the Breakers" was presented by local talent, followed later by other plays. In 1877 the club changed its name to "The As You Like It" club and presented a number of plays, the first of which was "Toodles," a domestic drama in two acts, and Betsy Baker, which played to a crowded house.

We copy a clipping taken from Mother Wright's scrapbook, taken from the local paper: "The Lake City Dramatic Club rendered 'Toodles' with the farce 'Betsy Baker' to a crowded house Wednesday evening. The cast was as follows: Toodles---W. W. Ferguson; Mrs. Toodles---Mrs. H. E. Wright; Farmer Acorn---J. W. Wilde; Mary Acorn---Miss Nellie Mendenhall; George Acorn---Will Griffith; Farmer Fenton---W. P. Keough; Charles Fenton---H. E. Wright; Lawyer Glib---I. W. Schiffer. Wright, Wilde and Griffith doubled parts, taking respectively---Policeman, Farmer 2 and Farmer 3. Betsy Baker cast: Betsy Baker---Miss Alla Mendenhall; Mr. Mouser---H. E. Wright; Mrs. Mouser---Mrs. H. E. Wright; Crummy---W. W. Ferguson.

"The rendition of both play and farce was much better than is usual upon the first appearance of amateurs. W. W. Ferguson would have made a good "Toodles" had he not forgotten some of his lines. Mrs. Wright had a splendid conception of Mrs. Toodles, and Miss Mendenhall was a capital Betsy Baker.

"We do not say this is discrimination—not at all. Certainly, as in all plays, some characters are more captivating and excite more admiration than others, and this is no exception. All the parts were fairly taken by the performers and we only speak the sentiments of the people when we say it was an interesting entertainment and will safely bear favorable criticism.

"The gross receipts were $63.25, will just about liquidate expenses. The club will probably present another play in several weeks and if a good house greets them a respectable sum will be secured for the bell fund, as the principal expense will be the music."

The bell fund referred to was the money being raised to purchase a fire bell, which was later purchased and is still in use.

The next play put on by this club was "Uncle Robert" and the paper had this to say: "The Histronics played to a full house Monday night and did better in every respect than on the previous occasion. 'The Limmerick Boy' was well played, Mr. Roberts as Paddy Miles' Boy, winning round after round of applause. His scene in Widow Fidgett's parlor as the Irish woman, was unusually good. Harry Wright and his wife were up in their lines and deserve all the compliments they received.

"In 'Uncle Robert' the Misses Mendenhall had good conceptions of their parts and were quite arch. Billy Keogh knew his lines well and acted up pleasantly. The orchestral music was good. Following are the casts: Limmerick Boy---Paddy Miles' Boy, W. L. Roberts; Harry, Harry Wright; Dr. Coates, James Wilde; Reuben, W. W. Ferguson; Jobe,

Wm. Griffith; Mrs. Fidget, Mrs. H. E. Wright; Jane Fidget, Mrs. J. J. Frank; Uncle Robert, W. L. Roberts; Grampus, W. W. Ferguson; Edward, Wm. Griffith; William, Wm. Keogh; Brownjohn, James Wilde; Louise, Nellie Mendenhall; Pattie, Alla Mendenhall."

The William Keogh in these casts was the stepson of Mat Elbert, an early-day pioneer. He later became a member of the famous Kempton Komedy Kompany, and with that company came often to Lake City. The *Lake City Phonograph* of November 2, 1907, carried the following: "The Kempton Komedy Kompany held the boards at the Armory Hall here three nights this week and that their entertainments were enjoyed is evidenced by the large audience at each performance. The plays were new and the scenery attractive. Keogh, the comedian of the company, is a former Lake City boy, and on account of his popularity is always given a cordial welcome here."

By 1877, Lake City boasted two pianos. One belonged to Mrs. J. W. Brockett and the other to Col. George Gardner.

In 1878, a group of men organized an orchestra at White Cross, and made their own instruments. A member of this group, H. E. Wright, made a banjo, the bottom of which was from a black powder can covered with a tanned groundhog skin. The wooden parts were whittled out of native wood. It remained in our family until December, 1962, when we donated it to the State Museum, where it may now be seen. A cornet band was organized in 1880, of which H. E. Wright was also a member.

Various other entertainment clubs were formed as the years passed. We found this program in the *Lake City Times*, dated March 30, 1893:

Program
Lake City Literary Club

Music---Male Quartet
Reading---Miss Talliaferro
Dialog---Six in Cast
Recitation---Mrs. Farrell
Debate---"Resolved that the Press is of more benefit than the Pulpit"
        Affirmative: G. W. Crowe, James Elmendorf
        Negative: R. E. Penniston, Ralph Whinnery
Speech---George Wilson
Music---Miss Mendenhall
Essay---Ray Madison
Duet---Mrs. G. W. Crowe and Mrs. Charley Whitmore.

Names familiar to many appeared in a program published in November of 1882. This was another entertainment given to add to the bell fund. Names listed on this program were Misses Fannie and Alla Mendenhall, F. M. Mendenhall, Walter Beam, W.H. Crooke, Mrs. Mignolet, Charles Blume, C.F. Hilgenhaus, Carl Patz, Miss Blood, T. K. Wonderly. A dodger advertising this musical is still in the possession of Mrs. Nettie Mendenhall, whose late husband was the son of F.M. Mendenhall and brother of Alla and Fannie.

Mother Wright told of concerts given over the telephone in 1881, folks from Silverton, Ouray, Capitol City, Rose's Cabin and Lake City taking part. The *Silver World* of October 1, 1881, gave an account of one such concert. D. W. Bates was the Lake City telephone operator at the time and those taking part were: W. Champlain at Rose's Cabin, the Silverton choir, Charles Acams of Mineral Point, C. F. Hilgenhaus, William Kellogg and W. P. Harbottle from Lake City.

We found an account of another concert in the October 15 issue of the *Silver World* of 1881 which said:

"An inteesting experiment was made last Sunday evening. Mr. Bates was at the Lake City instruments and Mrs. Lee at those of her residence in Capitol City. They sang several duets and then Mr. Bates called Rose's Cabin, Silverton and Ouray stations. From Silverton came roses and from Ouray, Mr. Al Long said he would join in—all sang several popular songs and so accurately that it seemed as if all were singing from the same book. Then an employe of Mr. Lee's saw mill up the north fork of Henson Creek played several airs on the accordian and a Silverton man played accompaniments to vocal music on the violin."

A club known simply as the Lake City Club was organized in 1890. The club rooms were on the second floor of the Armory. There were two large rooms, one of which was used for pool and billiards, and the other with tables for lunches and whist (then the popular card game). The opera house downstairs was used for plays put on by the club. Most of the money raised by the plays was given to the various community projects. The club expenses were financed by dues. Once a month the club had "Ladies Night." There were twenty-five active members of this club, which disbanded in 1900.

In 1901 the operetta "Queen Esther" was put on by the Baptist Church, assisted by most of the community. The cast of characters includes many who will be remembered by the readers. They are:

King Ahasuers, W. J. Nourse; Queen Esther, Mrs. Uglo; Mordecai, John Uglo; Haman, M. B. Milne; Zeresh, Florence Uglo; Prophetess, Minnie Griffiths; Harbonah, F. B. Hough; Herald, W. C. Humphry; Scribe, B. F. Cummings; Haman's child, Nan Milne and Daisy Ramsey; Princesses, Pearl Hunt, Eliza Wiers, and Nettie Uglo; King's Pages, Watson Avery and Glen Ogle; Queen's Pages, Ruth Edgerton and Edna Beam; King's Guards, E. F. Calvin and V. K. Ramsey; Court Guards, Charles Holroyd and Fred Davidson. Chorus: Mesdames George Richards and V. K. Ramsey; Misses Myrtle O'Brian, Hilda Isaacs, Myrtle Maurer, Louise Mayer, Helen Dorland, Minnie Griffiths, Pearl Hunt, Eliza Wiers, Nettie Uglo; Messrs. O. C. Ramsey, Taylor Ray, Ernest Mendenhall, F. B. Hough, Roy Rigney, J. E. Allen, Will Keelor, John Maurer Jr., and W. J. Nourse.

In 1909 a dramatic club was organized by Marian Hoffman and her cousin Miriam Bowman. Marian was the daughter of the pioneer Dr. D. S. Hoffman.

The only play put on by this group was "Eager Heart," but the club met after that as a social club and had many happy times. Members of that club still living are Mrs. Edna Hoffman, Mrs. Ruth Vernon, Mrs. Carolyn Wright, all of Lake City; Mrs. Helen Richards, of San Diego, California; Mrs. Lucy Beam, of Cortez and Lake City; and Mrs. Gladys Forney, of Brighton, Colorado. These ladies get together whenever possible and have a wonderful time reminiscing.

The next series of home talent plays were given by the Green Basketball Team and their wives to raise money for repairing the Armory—which they did, in a splendid way. Their first play was "The Cheerful Liar," a comedy in three acts: I, Deception; II, Detection; III, Destruction. The cast included: Ralph Horton, now with the Public Utilities in Denver; Lyman Ready, now working in the Post Office in Denver; Raymond Dotts, deceased; Nathan Knowlton, deceased; C. E. Wright, Hinsdale County Welfare Director; Nadine Milne, now of California; Carolyn Wright, retired teacher; and Aileen Ready of Denver.

A number of fund-raising plays have been given through the years by the Ladies Aid and lodges. However, since T.V. no one seems to have the interest in home talent plays as in former years.

The Pioneer Jubilee Woman's Club was organized in Lake City in April, 1940, joined the State Federation in May, 1940, and the General Federation in September of the same year. This club is still going and merits much praise. It bought an old building, repaired and remodeled it into a beautiful club hall where its meetings are held. It put in a library and is now in the process of building a museum which, when finished, will be a credit to the Club, Town, and County.

In 1946, the Club sponsored a playground across the street from the hall on lots that had been donated for a park. The ladies cleaned the lots, put up swings for the children, made picnic tables, and furnished trash cans. Fourth of July celebrations are now held each year at this park.

The first officers elected in 1940 were, president, Mrs. L. W. Grandon; vice-president, Mrs. L. T. Beam; secretary, Mrs. C. H. Harkness; treasurer, Mrs. H. T. Hoffman. The present officers are, president, Mrs. L. W. Grandon; vice-president, Mrs. Elizabeth Ray; secretary, Mrs. J. M. Wells; treasurer, Mrs. L. C. Ely. The Pioneer Jubilee Woman's Club started with about twenty members and now has almost fifty.

With the exception of the years of depression, from the earliest years there has been an active Chamber of Commerce. Then there was the Boosters' Club some years back, composed of the leading business men who, true to their name, boosted morale, business, and pleasure.

The present Chamber of Commerce has done much to keep Hinsdale County alive. While there is still some mining going on and there are still hopes for a substantial revival of the prosperous mining days, the tourist business is the principal industry and people come from all parts of the world to enjoy their vacations in this Switzerland of America, with its beautiful mountains, lakes and streams, good fishing, good hunting, and friendly people.

Another recreation of the early days, and one which folks hope to renew, was roller skating, which was enjoyed by young and old. Describing it best are some of the articles found in some of the old newspapers. The October 24, 1884 edition of the *Mining Register* had this to say: "Lake City has a very bad case of skating rink fever. Must be food for the Gods—small Gods—to get off in a safe corner, and watch Downey and John Bell do the grapevine." And another article in the same paper read: "Tomorrow night Tom Beam and Col. Stirman are expected to skate a race. Squire Brown will appear tonight as usual in his graceful 'Feets.'

"Joe Carrol is a great favorite with the ladies. He helps the young and old alike in the most bewitching manner.

"Leon Le Fevre is quite a beau. His strong arm supports many a nervous lady and helpless girl. Mayor Bill and Tom Stanley will appear in several new cuts and fandangoes."

And in the October 31 edition of the same paper we read under the heading "The Rink":

"As John Risse used to find great pleasure in the Hole-in-the-wall, so many of our citizens find pleasure in the skating rink, and the crows continue to pour into the Opera House every night. As soon as Tom Beam completes his concentrator, which is now absorbing all his time, he will challenge Bob Rogers."

Later, ice skating was enjoyed by the community under the direction of the Lake City Skating Club. At the north end of Silver Street, between Seventh and Eighth Streets, the block was flooded by the use of the fire hydrant on the corner of Seventh and Silver. A small house was erected on the edge of the rink where skates could be put on and taken off by a huge pot-bellied stove. Benches lined the walls. Electric lights were strung down the center of the rink, and night skating was popular. Many came just to watch, as there were many accomplished fancy skaters. At times hockey was

Folks did not sit around the fire in the house in the earlier days in the wintertime, but enjoyed many winter sports. Besides ice skating, coasting was a popular sport, enjoyed by young and old. When there was snow on the ground, coasting, sleighing and bobsled riding were popular sports. There were many places to coast. The most popular hills for the bobsleds were Crooks Hill and Baptist Hill. The main road up Crooks Hill was almost straight up from the Texan Resort Motel, one mile south of Lake City. The present blacktop road was not then constructed. The larger sleds were quite heavy and a mule was used to pull the sleds up the hill. The most used hill for the younger children was the Baptist Hill, north of the Baptist Church on Fourth and Bluff Streets. Sometimes a track was broken up above the old Abbot house (now owned by H. L. Townsend), west of Bluff Street back of the Hoffman house. One could go from the top of this hill, past the Baptist church and on down the Fourth Street hill, across Silver Street and often as far as Gunnison Avenue. Sometimes single sleds were used with several on a sled, other times the youngsters would go down "belly-buster." There was usually a large bonfire to warm by and occasionally toast marshmallows.

Baseball became a popular sport in the early 1900's. Prior to that time the school kids had their own forms of ball, called one old cat and two old cat and cross out. Then a young negro, nephew of Willis Williams, came to town from Kansas City, where he had been playing baseball. He was a pitcher and threw the first curve ball that had been seen in this area. He soon had a bunch of recruits anxious to become pitchers. Then a barber named Tytus, who was also a curve pitcher, came to town; a dentist, Will Butler, from Pennsylvania; and still another, from Louisiana, named Jona Hobson.

C. E. Wright, pitcher of the Lake City Blues.

The Green Basketball Team—Western Slope Champions, 1921. Left to right: Mathew Kinney, Frank Wright, Paul Ramsey, Ralph Horton, Henry Hoffman, Clarence E. Wright, and John Milne.

With their coming, interest in baseball really started. Practice started at the school grounds in the evening, and on Sunday afternoons they met across the river on the flat later known as the ball park. Usually sides were chosen by pre-appointed captains.

With the arrival of Vick Eckdall, a meat cutter from Kansas City and a real ball player, a ball team was organized known as the Blue Team. Aid was solicited from the business men of the town and the team soon had the support and finances to look for material for the making of a real team. Eckdoll was elected captain and manager. He acquired Grayson, a pitcher from the Kansas City Blues and Sissiler, catcher, who were both given employment by the business houses. Then came the Carroll brothers, Pete and Antone, who were hired to play first base and left field. Eckdoll held down second base. Will Humphries and Walter Mendenhall, both home boys, were the other outfielders. Jim Pate from the Yellow Medicine mine was shortstop. William Rawson, who had come here from Kansas City, had the "hot corner" at third base. Other players were Dugan Smith and Denison Fuller.

The Lake City Blues were members of the league consisting of Salida, Gunnison, Montrose, Delta, Olathe and Grand Junction. The Blues did not lose a single game. Later when there was not enough support to have a paid team, the Lake City Blues were composed of all local boys. C. E. Wright was the local pitcher. Baseball died out when this group got too old to play.

In 1920 basketball became the pastime for the winter months. Games were played in the old Armory, now called the City Hall. Married men played against the singles, civilians played against the soldiers. Even the women got into the game and organized the married women against the single girls. In November the men's team scheduled a game against the high school team, who later went to State for the playoffs. The town team had only met a few times and had no suits. They were beaten by the Gunnison High School, who were coached by Mr. Krause of the Gunnison Normal, now Western State College. After this the bunch got down to real practice, secured new suits, green for the first team and red for the second. In the spring of 1921 the Green Team, as they were now known, played Gunnison Normal, here and in Gunnison. They played Montrose, Delta, Olathe, Ouray, Gunnison High and Telluride town team. This game was in Lake City for the championship of the Western Slope town teams. After five minutes overtime the Green Team won 43 to 38. It was later discovered that some of the officials had bet on the Telluride team. No games were lost by the Green Team. Seven members

Old Timers' party at the home of Mrs. Ruth Vernon.

Pupils of Lake City school, celebrating the birthday of William Wright on a sleigh ride to Bakers for dinner. A. A. Baker, driver of the the four-horse team, is the youngest son of the D. C. Bakers.

of the original Green Team are still living. They are Ralph Horton, now with the P.U.C. in Denver; Paul Ramsey, Durango; Mathew Kinney, retired newspaper man, Denver; John Milne, Arlington, California; Henry Hoffman and C. E. Wright, still living in Lake City.

During the early 1900's there was an interest in racing, and a quarter mile circular track was built on the east side. This track was used for both horse racing and bicycles. Lawn Marine had the fastest pacing horse and Lucious Talliferro was the leading man on wheels. They once had a race between a horse and cycle. The horse won in the short distance and the wheel in the mile.

This was the time of the Booster Club, and they also added to activities out of town in the form of boats and boat races on Lake San Cristobal.

It was also about this time that Brint Ramsey boasted of having ridden his bicycle across the top of Uncompaghre Peak. We never did learn how Brint got the bicycle TO the top of the peak—he must have carried it up the incline from the foot, but tracks proved that he had ridden across the top.

The story of early-day entertainment in Lake City would not be complete without the description of the Sunday School picnic held at the Baker ranch in the grove south of the ranch. Everyone was invited and special rates were given for those wishing to go down on the train. Some drove with horse and buggy, others rode horseback, and many children rode their burros.

Separate lunches were prepared which were all spread out around large tablecloths brought from the ranch for the occasion. Mother Baker always furnished the ice cream—gallons of it, made of almost pure cream and frozen in a hand-turned freezer. No one, but NO ONE has ever made ice cream like that made by dear Mother Baker. We can see her smiling yet as she handed out the generous dishes to the boys and girls.

Dad Baker and the boys always put up a merry-go-round, drawn by a horse, which was enjoyed by young and old. After lunch different games were played. When the train whistle was heard we knew the picnic was over and all hurried to get ready to leave.

This picture includes many of the pioneers written about in our book. It is a picture taken at the Baker VC Bar Ranch to celebrate either a birthday or an anniversary. Seated on the bottom row are, left to right: Mrs. W. P. Hunt, W. P. Hunt, D. C. Baker, Mrs. Baker, daughters Nettie and Elsie Baker and the four Hardy children, cousins of Mrs. Baker. Others in the picture are: Mr. and Mrs. W. S. Whinnery, Mr. and Mrs. George Richards, Mr. and Mrs. Buel R. Wood, Mr. and Mrs. T. L. Beam, Mr. and Mrs. J. A. Hunt, Sr., Mr. and Mrs. Kinney, Mrs. Donnel, Mr. and Mrs. William Green, Mr. and Mrs. William Hardy, Mr. and Mrs. E. G. Faires, sons Orville and Wilbur Baker, Dr. and Mrs. B. F. Cummings, and Lis Swisher.

LODGES AND THE PITKIN GUARD

The first lodge in Lake City was the IOOF. They received their charter for the Silver Star Lodge October 10, 1876. The lodge hall was on the Brockett Hall on Third and Gunnison. This building burned in 1888 and the lodge moved to the IOOF Hall, adjoining the Christian Hall, where the post office now is located. The Deborah Rebekah lodge received their charter September 2, 1892. The lodge remained at this location, where they were when the charter was recalled. The IOOF obtained land for the IOOF cemetery and graded, fenced, and maintained the cemetery until the time of their decline. They also laid the cornerstone of the Hinsdale County Court House.

Members of the Masonic Lodge from other places who located here met in Brocketts Hall in 1875 and proposed the establishment of a Masonic Lodge.

Crystal Lake Lodge #34, AF and AM received their charter October, 1878. The Eastern Star was granted charter September, 1898. For many years after moving from the Brockett Hall, the lodge held their meetings in the Hough block, upstairs, and then moved to their present location on Silver Street.

The Independent Order of Red Men was established in Lake City in 1897. Their hall was located between Bluff and Silver Street on Second. Their membership dropped off and the lodge was discontinued in 1925. The Pocahontas, Woman's Auxiliary, was not until 1907. The costumes of both men and women were of Indian design and very attractive.

GAR was organized in 1883 with sixteen members. As time passed, the membership decreased until there were a very few left. One of the last active members was Dick James, who spent some time getting headstones for all known soldiers buried in either cemetery. At the time of his death there was not a grave here that did not have a stone from the government if there was any record of the deceased having served his country.

The Ancient Order of United Woodmen was granted charter in 1894 in the IOOF Hall on Gunnison Avenue. The membership increased rapidly and they were able to purchase the Christian Hall across the street from the IOOF Hall. The women's auxiliary was the Degree of Honor and was organized in 1898. The Christian Hall was a two-story building with the lodge upstairs and the dance hall on the ground floor. In connection with the AOUW lodge there was a side degree that was given the new members. One such initiation into the Degree of Old Cyrus was the initiation of Danny O'Neil. The event took place in the lodge room and Mr. O'Neil told me afterwards that he was sure that he was branded for life. He was blindfolded, bound to a table, chest bared, and branded on the chest with the letters AOUW. The branding was done with an icicle marking out the letters at the same time that a hot poker was drawn across a piece of fat meat close enough that Danny could hear it sizzle. The victim was unbound, blindfold taken off, and shirt put on. And a good time was had by all. AOUW surrounded their charter in 1910 and the members retained their insurance in the Modern Woodmen and Women of Woodcraft.

Information is to the effect that the Charter of the Silver Star Lodge N. 27 of Lake City, was taken up by Grand Master Carlstrom on July 24, 1953, evidence being to the effect that its total membership the past several terms had reached a low of ten, that only four thereof maintained their residence in Lake City and that they were away most of the time.

No. 27 was instituted under the dispensation granted by Grand Master C. P. Dunbaugh and the charter members were John Swanson, Peter A. Simmons, W. A. McGinnis, C. B. Hickman, John F. Dodds, and E. N. Campbell, all of whom were admitted on cards; John Davis was an inititate member and two more were admitted on card, giving a total membership of nine on date of institution. Term report of December 31, 1876, showed a total of 27 contributing members.

Lake City at its height had a population of 4000 when all branches of the order were represented: Silver Star Lodge No. 27, Deborah Rebekah Lodge No. 18, Golden Rule Encampment No. 12, and Canton Lake City No. 20. Only the Rebekah Lodge remains at this time.

Of the ten members identified with Lodge in its last report W. S. Whinnery had been a member for more than 61 years John Benson, 58 years; B. F. Cummings, 55 years. These three of the ten members were the only recipients of vetera jewels.

The Pitkin Guards was organized in 1878 with a member ship of 38. This Company C, 1st regiment, of the Colorad

National Guard, was organized for the protection of the area against the possible uprising of the Indians. However, there never was a cause for the action of the Pitkin Guards for this purpose. In 1879 the Guards were reorganized, with a new membership. New Springfield rifles, 45.79, black powder rifles with removable bayonets, were received with large boxes of ammunition for a troupe of 50 members. The Pitkin Guards remained active in the community for many years and entered into the amusements for themselves—and also for everyone else. These amusements were the Drum and Bugle Corps, Brass Band, and Rifle Range and Club which was located east of the Lake Fork River near the foothills. They had a 100- and 200-yard rifle range where they had regular target practice and it was open to the members whenever they wished to practice. All the ammunition was furnished by the Government, who encouraged members to become proficient in shooting and marksmanship. The best of the riflemen each year entered the State Shoot at Denver.

The demonstrations given by the Pitkin Guards were always well attended and enjoyed, as were the exhibitions given by the Drum Corps, who marched and performed on the streets for the amusement of the public. The troupe also gave marching and maneuvering performances whenever they were practicing. At times, while still in uniform, after practice they would assemble in the Armory and have contests with the public on the roller skating rink. Their brass band was always a drawing card and in the evenings there would be concerts on the streets.

First automobile in Lake City—owned by Thos. Beam and son L. T.

HOTELS

There were many hotels and rooming houses in the early days of this area, some of the halls having cots and double-decked bunks which were rented by the night at so much a bed. The first hotel of any size in the town was the American House established in 1876, located on Gunnison Avenue between Third and Fourth Streets. The lots are now in use as a tourist court. This structure was of frame, two and a half stories, with stairway and hall in the center, a kitchen and dining room downstairs and rooms from the hallway upstairs. The building was heated with large wood stoves and the toilets were all of the outside types and divided by a fence for the men and women. There was no insulation in the outer walls, so the rooms not having stoves were cold in the winter. This hotel was known throughout the San Juans. In 1900 the building was still standing, but in a rundown condition and not in use. Later it was destroyed by fire. In 1885 Samuel Haughland opened the American House on Fourth and Silver Street. Years later this became the Occidental Hotel. A spacious dining room and kitchen were on the lower floor. There were also a lobby with the usual pot-bellied stove in the center and some rooms on the lower floor at the south end. A stairway led to the rooms upstairs. In all, there were twenty-two rooms. From the second story some of the rooms facing the west opened on to a veranda over the sidewalk with a small fence on the outside. There were chairs and couches for the patrons.

Another old and well-known hotel was the Pueblo House, which was first operated by V. P. Flora in 1885. This hotel was located on the east side of Silver Street near the middle of the block between Third and Fourth Street. Some of the original equipment was still in the lobby in 1920. The south part of the dining room was of hewn logs and the floor joists were hewn logs. Later the logs were sided over and another room built on the north side. Also, another story was added, making it a two-story building. The front of this building was blistered from three fires. Across the alley there were two separate outdoor toilets for men and women. There were bowls and pitchers in each room for water and a slop jar for the dirty water in an enclosed wooden commode. Water was carried to rooms from a well. In the front of the building on the second floor there was a porch or balcony across the entire front over the sidewalk. This was a favorite place for the patrons to sit and enjoy the afternoon sun and chat. Adjoining the dining room on the ground floor was the bar, where all of the best liquor was displayed. Some, but not all, of the rooms had stoves for heat. There was a wood and coal range about seven feet in length with an oven large enough for a bake pan of about three feet by two feet. A part of the top was one piece about three by two feet where the steaks were fried.

Daniel T. McLeod and William Patterson operated the Pueblo Hotel in 1890. Later the hotel was operated by William Patterson and his wife Bridget. This dear Irish couple were dearly loved by all of the town and especially the school children, who called him "Uncle Billy." As Uncle Billy grew old he would sit in front of the hotel under the balcony with his chair tipped back against the wall and wait for the kids going to school. This was a very great event in his daily life. Each kid as he passed Uncle Billy would receive a nickel. Regardless of who the kids were, he knew their names and also their parents, who sometimes would not permit their girls and boys to take the gift from Billy. But they would be called back to him so that he could put the coin in their hand. Many of the kids then did not have a nickel to spend. There was a candy store on the corner going to school from the Pueblo House that did a good business from the many coins given to the children by Uncle Billy. Patterson and his wife became unable to take care of the hotel business so they took in a partner, Jimmy Sheridan. This partnership lasted until 1900 when the hotel was leased to John Allison. Patterson, his wife and their daughter, Ellen Graham, moved to their two-story building across the alley facing Gunnison Avenue where they still took care of some of their old patrons in their rooming house. Their last days were spent at this location.

W. W. Thompson opened the Silver Street American House on Third and Silver Street in 1897. At this date the American House on Gunnison Avenue had burned and the other American House on Fourth and Silver had been changed to the Occidental.

After Allison the Pueblo House changed hands to Mrs. L. Kelly, mother of Mrs. Nancy Burke, now County Treasurer since 1960. Then the hotel was leased by John Hammond and wife who operated the hotel until 1920. From 1920 for a number of years the hotel was not operated at all times. There were

Parlor of the Old Pueblo House.

Occidental Hotel. Three hotels by this name burned. Extreme left, Mrs. George Gardner.

several who tried to make a go of it but were not successful. Later, the main part of the hotel was torn down; now the only part of the famous hotel is the building where the Forbes Antique Shop is located. This was the last of early-day hotels. Mr. Hammond also had interests in the Hinsdale Mining and Development Company and at one time owned the Old Reece Richart Ranch, 11 miles south of Lake City, and sometimes called the Hammond Ranch. It is now the property of Jack Porter.

The Occidental Hotel was a well-known place to stay when in Lake City. It was located at two different locations and in three different buildings with a number of operators. In 1885, E. A. Thompson operated the Occidental Hotel, located on the west side of Silver Street between Third and Fourth Streets. Like the other hotels of this date, there was a veranda over the sidewalk across the front of the building. It was a two-story frame building with a large dining room and kitchen on the ground floor. It had fourteen rooms which were heated by wood and coal stoves. No modern facilities were used. Water came from a well by use of hand pump. After Mr. Thompson, who lost the hotel by fire, came Mrs. Propper, who rebuilt and later leased the hotel. Her husband worked in the Lake City Times office. Mrs. Propper later became the wife of General George F. Gardner. The Gardners once made their home at the corner of Sixth and Silver Street, which is presently the home of the authors of this book. After Mrs. Propper, D. T. McLeod bought the Occidental and had just moved in, fire destroyed the building. Mr. McLeod immediately rebuilt the hotel and furnished it throughout. Before the usual opening was held the third fire on the same lot destroyed the hotel. The loss was covered by insurance but Mr. McLeod did not wish to attempt another hotel at this location. He invested in the American House, formerly owned by Samuel Haughland, on the corner of Fourth and Silver Streets, where he again opened the Occidental Hotel. It was later sold to P. J. McPolin, who with his wife, Katherine, operated the hotel under the name of Occidental until they retired in 1937. The hotel was then sold to H. B. Grant, who was remodeling it at the time that it was destroyed by fire in the year of 1937.

The La Veta Hotel was located on the corner of Third and Gunnison Avenue adjoining the Whitmore Block. This was a two-story frame building with kitchen, dining hall and office on the ground floor. The sleeping rooms were upstairs. In 1895, T. Tomkins operated the hotel and he was followed by Mr. and Mrs. Whit Lowden, and in 1905 Mrs. L. Kelly took over the dining room. This hotel, like most of the others, was destroyed by fire when the Whitmore block burned.

There were hotels at White Cross, Sherman, Capitol City, Lake Shore and Rose's Cabin, but they were only small and not operated in the winter months.

Hotel at Rose's Cabin owned and operated by Mr. and Mrs. Charles Schafer.

First cabin at Rose's Cabin.

Sherman Hotel. Last building left standing at Sherman.

LAKES AND FISHING

For many years to get fish in this area was up to the people of the community. They had to secure the fish, see that they were properly planted and cared for. This was accomplished by different organizations and even individuals. It was almost impossible to get fish from the State hatcheries as the places with a larger population were always favored.

Fish from the federal hatcheries could be obtained after so much government "red tape." First the area had to request the proper forms through the Representatives and Senators. These forms had to show that the applicant was able to and would meet the fish on delivery and plant them immediately in the stream or lake designated on the application without expense to the government. The fish cans were usually taken by pack horses to the place of plant. Ice had to be placed in the cans and on a long pack trip the water had to be changed. On arrival at the place of planting the cans had to be slowly immersed into the water so that the temperature of the can and contents would equalize with the water in the lake or stream before the fish were liberated.

As far as known, there were always fish in the Lake Fork from Sapinero to Sherman when the first settlers came to this area. But there were no fish above Sherman according to the diary of H. E. Wright in 1877, who wrote that he and his partners frequently stopped at Sherman to fish to take fish with them to White Cross. There seemed to be some chemical in the water from certain ores in Cooper Creek which prevented the fish from going above Sherman, but by the time it reached Sherman it was diluted enough that the fish were no longer affected by it. The discoloration from Cooper Creek is still noticeable, but evidently not so strong, as there are no fish from Sherman through to the Park.

The beaver were a great help in getting fish to live through the winters, as they made dams where the fish could find water deep enough for protection. In shallow water the fish would freeze. There were beaver along most of the Lake Fork, but no evidence of them in Burrows Park, Cataract or Cottonwood. About the same time that the beaver moved into the White Cross area and built ponds opposite the Champion Mine, the boys working at the mine and on the county road volunteered to take fish to the ponds if the fish were available. This was arranged and in this way the beaver ponds were stocked. Native trout were stocked and in two years grew to one and three quarter pounds. When this was learned most of the fish were caught. The ponds and the stream were planted the third year but they did not remain in the stream as they did not stay in the stream until recently.

The Curao brothers stocked the North Henson stream many years ago, but like the White Cross area, the fish did not stay there. Later Ben and Abe Guinneau stocked the beaver ponds above the Gallic Vulcan, and the fish thrived and spawned and there are now fish all the way from Capitol City up North Henson above the Gallic Vulcan.

J. F. Steinbeck, an ardent fisherman, packed the first fish to Crystal Lake but they did not live as there was no sign of them the following year. He thought there might not be the right kind of feed. Later W. P. Hunt and his nephews Ben and Joe Hunt filed on the ground at Crystal Lake but their filing was denied. However, they did obtain a least on the lake and later on Water Dog Lake. They packed in fresh water shrimp to feed the fish they planted and the fish thrived and grew.

Crystal Lake and Crystal Peak towering above it were named from the beautiful crystals found on the eastern slope of the peak in what was called the Crystal Beds. A few crystals can still be found but most of the very beautiful ones have been taken by tourists.

Water Dog Lake was so named because of the number and size of the water dogs found there, some of which were a foot in length. These dogs are of the salamander family and are sometimes called hellbenders. They were quite numerous in the lake until the fish grew large enough to eat them. I have seen a three-pound trout with a water dog, too long to swallow, hanging out of his mouth. As the trout grew, however, the water dogs disappeared. This lake is especially known for its fine-eating fish and their size.

The cabins built by the Hunts in 1900 at both Crystal and Water Dog Lakes are still standing.

During the lease on these lakes fish were shipped to hotels in Denver and to the dining car service on the D&RG Railroad. I often went fishing with the Hunt brothers as they wanted the large fish caught from the lakes because the best marketing size for fish was two to three fish to the pound. The larger fish were hard to market and they also ate many of the smaller fish. These large fish were sold to hatcheries and small lakes for spawning stock.

Lake San Cristobal was for many years the principal source of Rainbow spawn. The fish were netted in the spring and stripped, the spawn packed in moss and ice and rushed to the federal hatchery at Creede, Colorado, where it was placed in troughs for hatching. A percent of the hatch was returned to Lake San Cristobal, and the rest shipped to other waters in the State. Later the Fish and Game Department, with the help of County machinery, built lakes in various parts of the County and successfully stocked some high lakes by airplanes. Cooper Lake and Cataract Lake are two of the high lakes so stocked.

Fish were packed into Larson Creek where there were beaver ponds deep enough to protect them, but the beavery ponds washed out during high water and the fish went with the water. Later the Fish and Game Department built ponds in the head of Larson where now there is very good fishing. There is still room in this area for more ponds.

Devil's Lake and a small lake at the head of Independence Gulch have both been stocked, but so far the fish have not thrived there.

In 1954 the Hinsdale County Chamber of Commerce decided to build lakes just over Slumgullion Pass to take care of the growing number of tourist fishermen. Some of the money was raised by selling Lake City Citizenship papers to the tourists. O. W. (Pat) Maloney, annual visitor from Tulsa, Oklahoma, bought the first one, for $25, and sold a number to his friends. This started the fund and twelve lakes were made. It was then suggested that anyone donating $100 or more could have a lake named after him. The following lakes were named: Lake Pat Maloney, Lake Hildegard, Lake Slug Stewart, Lake Frank Walker, Lake Art Weaver, Lake Emory Carper, and Lake Zeikli. Beautiful markers were set up with the names on them, but it was later learned that naming the lakes this way was illegal and the beautiful name signs were taken down. However, several of the better known lakes are still called by the original names.

Later the Fish and Game Department built a lake on Williams Creek, known as Williams Creek Lake. It is 3 miles north of Pagosa Springs but in Hinsdale County. It is a huge lake containing 342 acres. A couple of years later another large lake, known as the Rio Honda Reservoir, was built. Now added to the nickname of "Tiny Hinsdale," is the slogan "Hinsdale, the County of Lakes."

Boats on Lake San Cristobal about 1894.

Lake San Cristobal, where Arthur Chapman, author of "Out Where the West Begins," said, "Now I know where the West begins." Photo by W. H. Jackson.

A day's catch at Water Dog Lake, 1929.

LAKE SAN CRISTOBAL

Lake San Cristobal, the most beautiful and the largest natural body of water in the state of Colorado, was formed by what is known as the Slumgullion Slide. According to geologists, a huge geyser of mud formed some six hundred years ago and slid down the mountain much the same as lava flows from a volcano. The "break off" or starting point of the slide can easily be seen from the Slumgullion Road. This slide made a dam across the Lake Fork River, thus forming the lake. Engineers who have been studying the formation estimate that the slide is still moving at the rate of three inches a year. One proof of this is the leaning positions of the trees growing on the slide.

The so-called "mud," is really a clay, and when W. L. Bailey was principal of the Lake City High School he brought some of it down to school to experiment in clay modeling and found it very successful. I was in his art class and still have the vase I made of that clay in 1908. I have often wondered why no one else ever found a use for it.

Lake San Cristobal is four miles south of Lake City. It is three miles long and in the widest place one mile wide. Its waters pass on through a rocky canyon where the waters leap one hundred fifty feet. This place is called Argenta Falls. There is no more beautiful spot in nature than these falls, whose thunderings can be heard from afar and make eternal requiem of the five victims of Packer's fiendish atrocity, whose graves lie about a mile below.

It was on the banks of beautiful San Cristobal that Arthur Chapman, author of "Out Where the West Begins," stretched out his arms toward the sky and said, "Now I KNOW where the West begins."

Lake San Cristobal Fishing, as told by Julius Von Sinden, an early-day visitor to the San Juan:

"One of the most picturesque of the Rocky Mountain Lakes in Colorado, is Lake San Cristobal in the region known as the Silvery San Juan in the Southwestern part of the Centennial state. It was named in honor of the Spanish explorer of a century or two ago, by a member of Hayden's Geographical Survey, to whom the name was suggested by one of Tennyson's poems. It has local fame for its fine trout, to test which it was my privilege at the invitation of the 'Sage of San Cristobal' — as a retired prospector who had his shack on the lake shore was known. He was more familiarly called 'Doc,' having had an education back East for a physician, but did not follow his profession. He preferred to become a gold hunter and settled down to 'batch' by beautiful San Cristobal.

"As a newspaper man in quest of a vacation, I naturally sought such a host as Doc, and Doc was none the less proud to have as a guest 'one of them there newspaper fellers,' as he facetiously referred to such of my kind. "Doc" was Doctor Bothewell, who came here to prospect and liked it so well he decided to make it his home.

"One day I got a saddle horse in the little mining town of Lake Fork of the Gunnison River on a good wagon road. It led close to granite falls, irridescent with rainbows, past a ranch with verdant fields, and close by another set of falls, the Argenta, over which the waters fell in a mass of sunlit seething foam. At the end of a four-mile ride Doc's cabin was reached. It was of unpainted boards of two rooms, the front one containing supplies and a variety of fishing and prospecting equipment. The rear room did service for cuisine and parlor and was fitted with a couple of bunks. Boxes nailed to the walls did duty as shelves, where reposed magazines and periodicals in a profusion to delight any disciple of Isaac Walton, who wished to vary his piscatorial excursion with up-to-date reading when the weather or inclination invited intellectual recreation. Doc himself was a great reader. An ore-team going to the Golden Fleece mine brought up my valise, my horse was sent back to the stable, and I was installed 'for as long as I could stand it' at Doc's. It was a matter of several weeks, but a summary of my experiences will doubtless prove as interesting as details.

"Two of the summer months of the region are more or less rainy—the rains falling almost daily during July and August, showers being sometimes of hourly occurrence, and now and then a steady rain may fall for 24 to 36 hours.

"These were ideal days with a Mediterranean atmosphere, bright sunshine and deep blue skies, through which lazily sailed great fleecy clouds touched up with dazzling light. Soft breezes sighed through the spruce that clad the mountain slopes and anon broke the usually placid surface of the lake into ripples. On such days it suited me best to be in the shade of a birch reading a new summer novel: *Reveries*, *Three Men in a Boat*, *Arabian Nights*, *Grimm's Fairy Tales*, or some other old thing in that line, and looking up now and then to see the dragon flies dart back and forth on their wings of metallic sheen; then at sundown to row across the lake to a supper of trout fried in hot olive oil, served with watercress and broiled mushrooms, coffee par excellence and hot biscuits, and supplemented by a good-natured 'cussing' from Doc for being late. There were other days when the climate had its mountainous flavor with an air like wine—an atmosphere stimulating one to physical activity and when 'whipping' the lake was no hardship. The majority of the days were warm and sunshine and the nights always cool, so that at dark a fire was always welcome. We could read of the hot spells 'back East' with equanimity and pity the poor wretches whom circumstances did not permit the enjoyment of a sojourn at 9,000 feet altitude above sea level, in sight of perpetual snow, where the Dog Star raged and where refreshing sleep was always possible between woolen blankets.

"The fish in the lake comprise rainbow, native, and brook trout and their hybrids. It was a stocked lake, none of the finny tribe inhabiting it when white people came into the country, the falls not permitting the ascension of the trout from the river. Water-dogs alone occupied the lake and they were rapidly driven out by the trout which had been taken out of the stream below the falls and carted in barrels to San Cristobal. In that manner the stocking was begun.

"The trout multiplied rapidly and were prevented from leaving the lake by a screen placed across the lower end by Doc, who, with commendable public spirit, exercised a general supervision over the preserving. I found the trout very eccentric in their biting, it being necessary to employ a variety of artificial flies, the trout showing a wide range of preference to what they rose to. Their hours, too, for biting were very uncertain, but as there was always someone fishing at every hour of the day and night, it was no hard task to learn when and what they, the fish, took to. Sometimes it was grubs that lodged in decayed tree stumps, and which were obtained by hacking the stumps to pieces with an ax. At other times it was grasshoppers which were easily caught on the sunny mountain slopes. In fact, there was no trouble getting bait, the trouble lay in selecting the right kind and it was provoking to have the boat in which I stood surrounded by a beautiful array of the denizens of the deep inspecting the bait or fly, and then look up at me with an air that meant 'what does that chump take us for?' But when the right temptation was thrown to them it was a marvelous sight; the manner in which they fairly fell over each other in an effort to be the first to snap up the temptation. There were fishermen on the lake who instinctively knew what the fish were hankering for and such fishermen were looked up to with envy by less fortunate fishermen.

"There were several who rode up from town on their bicycles in the afternoon or evening and rode back after an hour or two with well filled baskets. Others came and went in carts or buggies. But one wants to live at the lake to get full enjoyment of the scenery; to see the gray pine squirrel at play and at dusk hear the mellow 'whoo whoo' of the spruce owl.

"In the fall of the year, when the quaker-asps [quaking aspens] begin to change the color of their leaves, there is some game to be had up in the hills. At one time it was very plentiful. The big-horn would be abundant today were it not for the failure of Colorado game laws to adequately protect mountain sheep. [The big-horns are now protected by law.] Now and then a deer [deer are still plentiful] is to be seen and occasionally a bob-cat. There is a 'varmint' or mountain lion, referred to by the Mexicans as el corcojow. It is a handsome creature, spotted[I have never seen "spots" on the now plentiful mountain lion] like a leopard and looks like a huge cat. It is powerful and bold in seeking food, but cowardly when menaced or attacked by man and dogs. Some elk are still to be found on the neighboring mesas. The accompanying picture shows one of the 'lordly' [a pet elk tamed by J. B. Michaels] in captivity in Lake City. Trappers occasionally get a fox, pine martin or lynx. Rabbits and ptarmigan are plentiful, and at Big Horse Park, at an altitude of 9,500 feet is a colony of prairie dogs around which hang a few coyotes. [Prairie dogs are found all over, not only in high altitudes.]

"The region around the lake was the home of grouse in large numbers but between hunters, hawks, ermine weasel and domestic cat they are almost gone.

"The woodchuck or ground hog is often met with above timber line [these animals are also seen in lower altitudes] and Doc told me of one with a pure white coat of fur being seen once on Engineer Mountain and also a family of albino chipmunks that made their home some four or five miles below the lake.

"An amusing incident took place at the lake one day in front of Doc's cabin. A woman in waders, one of a fishing party, had her skirts pinned up to keep them dry. She boldly entered the stream, rod in hand and cast for trout. Suddenly she screamed: 'Look at that snake! Look at that snake!' A harmless water snake had crawled from the opposite shore to a boom anchored across the stream to keep boats from going down the rapids and the lady fisherman in real fright, frantically flung her rod about. While her attention was riveted on the snake, a trout made a leap at the fly and the hook caught the fish in the back. This was a new predicament and now she screamed 'Look at that fish! Look at that snake!' in repetition in her excitement while she danced up and down in the water while the spectators roared with laughter. She pointed at the snake with one arm while with the other she swung the rod from which dangled the trout in imminent danger of having its back yanked out, and Doc accommodatingly lifted the trout out with a dip-net. Never was a fish caught in such mirth provoking circumstances.

"Near the lake are productive mines of ruby, silver, argentiferous, grey, copper and gold bearing telluride ores, and its waters also wash the 'slumgullion,' as a deposit of ashes from the crater of an extinct volcano is called; the environs of the San Cristobal thus affording ample resources for studying geology and mineralogy. Nor did I neglect botanizing as a nice collection of alpine flowers will bear witness."

Lake San Cristobal, subject of the foregoing article, has been pronounced by a number of world travelers as one of the three most beautiful bodies of mountain water on earth. It has most entrancing surroundings for camping, fishing, picnicking and fish frying.

Slumgullion "break off" that formed Lake San Cristobal. Photo by Rial Lake.

Lake San Cristobal
by Ray Madison

I had my birth when Vulcan's eqrthquakes tore
A mighty mountain to its fiery core,
And when it damned a busy river's flow
Through a deep canon it had cut below----
The scars, erosion vainly tries to hide,
Show yet, upon the mountains' side.

Ages, untold, I lay in placid ease,
Known only to the birds, the beasts and trees;
I knew not when the human race began,
And, yet had never mirrored face of man;
Unconscious of the Great Creator's aim
To make a being worthy of such name.

Many men, since then have come to me
Seeking proof of immortality,
And to the few who, unafraid, can dream,
I whisper, secretly the Master's scheme
Of making nature's beauties so divine,
That men are lured to follow His design.

As in a mirror, with frame in bas-relief,
My surface gleams and glistens far beneath
The towering mountains, from whose fountain-head
Burst forth the crystal streams by which I am fed--
Draw near! Look deep into my depths, O, man,
If measure of the deeds you've done, would'st scan.

There is magic in the spell I weave,
I heal the broken hearts of those who grieve,
And added tempo to the song, I bring
Of those, who in the joy of life, would'st sing----
Mayhap the small are great, and the great are small,
When they're imaged in Lake San Cristobal.

Men mined for gold along my rugged shore,
And babbled loudly, when they found rich ore;
Thought not of wealth, that will outlive the grave,
That contemplation of my beauty gave,
And, now a horde of men come here to play
Since mining of ore streaks ceased to pay.

In my unmeasured depths a spirit dwells
That soothes the tired mind and unrest quells;
I have an aspect for each need or mood;
The load that would'st thy weary soul enthrall,
Will disappear at Lake San Cristobal.

This lovely poem was given to me by the author several years before his death, with his permission to use it should I ever write a book.

Ray Madison was the son of two of Lake City's oldest pioneers. He graduated from the Lake City High School in 1898. His first wife was the daughter of Mr. and Mrs. George Vernon, also pioneers. He has two children, Ray and Kathleen. His wife, Alice, and his daughter, Kathleen, both went to school with me. He was a well-known newspaperman and an accomplished musician. A number of his poems have been published.

Packing ties at the V C Bar Ranch

Pet elk, owned by J. B. Michaels, was "bulldogged" by Leon LeFevre when he got out of the pen.

CRIME

From the earliest years in all mining camps, there came some people of the type not to be desired. Lake City was no different; however, the *Mining Register* of January 1, 1881, had this to say: "Its status is far above the average of Western and frontier cities, and no mining camp in the world can boast of more intelligent, cultured, and peaceful citizenship. A street brawl is of the rarest occurrence and for months the log cabin that serves for a calaboose is tenantless. The miners, not only of Lake City, but of the entire San Juan area are, as a general thing, intelligent, industrious, and ambitious. There is too much activity here for drones and the 'loafer' is not known. Nearly every miner has a prospect or two of his own into which he puts his earnings."

One author, in writing of Lake City, said that theft was the most prevalent crime. On this we do not agree, although at one time horse thieves threatened the peace of the community. A certain amount of petty thievery went on as always, but the fact remains that from the earliest times no miner locked his cabin. On the contrary, he usually left staple groceries, such as coffee and beans, so that a traveler could come in, stop to rest and eat. It was customary for the visitor to leave a note of thanks, the date, and his name. We can't leave our homes open today and expect to find anything on our return.

About the horse stealing, there seems to have been several reasons—or rather, excuses—given. One was that, unsuccessful in mining, someone would want to leave and "borrowed" a horse to get out of town. Of course the main reason had to be the man was a thief. This led the *Silver World* of August 7, 1875 to print: "We are not particularly fond of violence, but we do not know anything that would afford our citizens more pleasure than the hanging of a horse thief."

A crime of a different nature was committed about this time when a newcomer to the camp slashed a man in the back with a knife. There was talk of hanging, but instead the man was taken to Del Norte to jail and later fined for assault and battery. It was later discovered that there was an organized band of horse thieves in the country and a posse was sent out to get them. The men were caught and lodged in a temporary jail, but escaped when the sheriff who went to get them was shot by the guard, who mistook him for an intruder. This happened in April, 1876. It was then decided that the town needed a jail and by June a log building was completed but was far from adequate. The *Silver World* called it a "log calaboose" and the name stuck through the years.

A billiard hall was the scene of another murder that year when Dan Emmet shot John Roche and wounded another man. Emmet was arrested and released, was later arrested on another charge, and escaped by digging out of jail. The *Silver World*, disgusted with the way the law was handled, stated that he probably would have been found "not guilty" anyway.

In April, 1877, William Brock and Tom King "shot it out" on Silver Street. King was hit first, but returned fire and hit Brock twice. King died and Brock was acquitted.

Election arguments more than once brought on murder. One such argument led to the death of Luther Rhea, who had argued with Jack Wells over the election of J. W. Hughs. Wells harbored a grudge over the argument, walked into the Centennial Saloon and deliverately shot Rhea. The funeral for Rhea was conducted by Reverend George Darley. Wells was acquitted, much to the disgust of everyone who knew both men.

Another election argument was settled with guns in November, 1881, when J. C. Young shot Frank Bennet, candidate for county clerk. Young pleaded "not guilty" and was released.

A double shooting which shook our community in 1901 was that of John Addington and Alex Surtees. The two men had quarreled over a woman of questionable character and had earlier in the day had a fist fight. They met on Main Street in front of the Hough building where they began shooting at each other. Surtees dropped dead in the street while Addington ran into the yard adjoining the building and into the "Chick Sales" building, where he was found.

Mrs. Emma Mayers and daughters ran a rooming house on the second floor of the building and had just washed sheets, hanging them on the clothes line in the yard below. Addington, while running through the yard splattered blood all over the sheets.

Addington was taken to the newly opened hospital where he died the following morning. Both victims were married men. Addington had several children.

Two young ladies, who had been passing the laundry of "John Chinaman," as he was called, heard the shots and backed into the doorway of the laundry. John, wanting to protect the girls, lifted the curtain below the ironing board, which concealed a bed where the laundry men took turns sleeping, and pushed them into the bed. Then he called his helper and both men also dived into the bed, where they all huddled together until they hard voices outside. John stuck his head out and then crept to the window. All seemed to be well so he called to the others. The two girls were often teased about being in bed with the Chinamen, but they did not mind, and were very grateful to John.

I, Clarence Wright, lived just a half block from where this shooting took place, and was coming from the woodshed with a load of wood when I heard the shooting. I dropped the wood and ran to the scene to see Billy Renshaw and Retti Ray carrying Addington, and Surtees lying dead.

A promising young doctor, R. O. Lacy, son of the pioneer Dr. R. O. Lacy, Sr., walked into a saloon while intoxicated and shot his best friend, Henry Vittle, for no reason whatsoever. Because he was drunk, he was sentenced to only a year in the county jail and was allowed to go out and see his patients when he was needed.

Patrick Donelen, a saloon keeper at Capitol City, shot and killed Anton Nickoli, a man who came into his saloon and started an argument. He was sentenced to a number of years in the penitentiary at Canon City. I was on the same train that took him out, and I remember that although my father, W. P. Hunt, was the sheriff with him, I was terrified at the thought of being on a train with a murderer.

Another shooting I remember was that of a man who was shot because he had interfered when a man was beating his wife. I remember that this man served twenty years in Canon City and that he did not live long after he was released.

In 1908 another election shooting took place here in a saloon. Dr. B. F. Cummings, a Democrat, went into a saloon and was bragging on the outcome of the election, when Steve Kinsey, a Republican, started an argument about the legality of the election. Kinsey claimed at his trial that Cummings had started toward him with a billiard cue, and that he HAD to shoot as he was a small man and Cummings a large one. At the next term of District Court, with Judge Shackleford presiding, the jury rendered the verdict of guilty of assault with intent to commit murder. While he was being held in the county jail, a drunk by the name of Kit Carter, passed him some whiskey and a gun. When the deputy went to feed him, Kinsey, by this time very drunk, pulled the gun and shot the deputy. J. A. Hunt, Jr., in the hip. Had it not been for this last shooting, Kinsey might have gotten off with a light sentence, but he got no sympathy after that and was sent to the penitentiary. Kit Carter was jailed for his part in the affair and while serving time in the log jail was burned to death. It is thought he kicked over the lamp, starting the fire.

One crime in 1876 that should be noted was the embezzlement of $40,000 from the First National Bank. Harry McIntire had come from Saguache to open a branch bank. He had come highly recommended as an upright and honest man and the Saguache paper had said that Lake City was very lucky to get him. In 1880 he was convicted of embezzling the $40,000.

There were several lynchings in the early days, the first of which was the hanging of Billy Le Roy, and three other outlaws for robbing the Lake City stage in 1881.

The road at that time was a never-ending climb. The Barlow and Sanderson stages conveyed passengers and mail to the railroad at Del Norte. Billy Le Roy was a notorious desperado, who had been arrested for a similar crime before and had escaped while being taken to prison. He came back to Colorado with his criminal friends who in May, 1881, tried to hold up the Lake City stage but were unsuccessful in that they frightened the horses and they ran away. Then on the night of the 18th, the outlaws again lay in wait on the Divide between Mirror Lake and Antelope Springs. When the stage came along they fired into it, wounding one passenger. They robbed the occupants of the coach of their valuables, took the mail and express sacks and ordered the driver to go on.

A reward was offered for their capture and a search followed. They were soon captured and taken to Del Norte. The sheriff was seized and bound and the prisoners were taken to a clump of trees and hanged. After a half hour their bodies were taken down and placed back in their cells. This was the last road agent activity on the Slumgullion road.

The next lynchings were those of Betts and Browning, the story of which is told in another place. Another shooting is also told in the story of "Hell's Acres."

Some old-timers remember tales of "Billy the Kid," the ruthless young killer of the Pecos country and his band of thieves and cutthroats who used to ride through the town "shooting it up." We have no knowledge that they ever killed anyone here.

A mail carrier named Hoag, who with his partner had been carrying mail between Lake City and Sapinero, once came in with empty sacks, claiming that he had been held up. An immediate investigation showed that there were no tracks around the place he claimed he had been held up, but his own. We never did learn what became of him, but he was always referred to as "the man who held himself up."

Packer Club Card

Site of the Packer Massacre showing graves of the murdered men. Hundreds of tourists visit these graves every year.

PACKER THE CANNIBAL

Hinsdale County was the scene of the most gruesome crime that was ever committed.

A few miles from Lake City may be seen an iron fence and a marker bearing the names Israel Swan, George Noon, Shannon Bell, Frank Miller and James Humphreys.

These men, with Alfred Packer, had started on a prospecting trip in the fall of 1873. They stayed in Ouray for several weeks and then left in February against the
advice of Chief Ouray, who had tried to help them. Packer with his five companions went on into the winter-bound country of the San Juan. Six weeks later Packer appeared alone at the Los Pinos agency on Cochetopa Creek. He said he had been separated from his companions five days after they left Ouray camp and said they may have gone on to Silverton. He told a grim tale of wandering and starving in the winter-bound mountains, but those who saw him said he looked too fat and healthy for a starved man. The fact that his first request was for whiskey instead of food added to the evidence that later convicted him. He seemed to have plenty of money and did a great deal of bragging while drinking which aroused suspicion. When asked to go with a hunting party to look for the men, he agreed and started out with the hunting party, but part way he refused to go farther. He was seen throwing something in a stream they crossed and investigation proved it to be the wallets of the dead men. He finally admitted killing Bell and pleaded self defense. The bodies were later found, four of them in a row and the fifth, Bell, apart from the others. Packer escaped and was hunted for nine years.

When he was located in Wyoming, living under an assumed name, he was arrested, brought to Denver and placed in the Arapahoe jail. He was later brought to Lake City, where he was tried April 13, 1889, convicted of murder, and sentenced to be hanged on the 19th of May. Because of a technicality in the law, he won a new trial and a change of venue to Gunnison County. There he was sentenced to forty years at hard labor at the State Penitentiary at Canon City by Judge Harrison in 1886.

There were many tales told about the sentencing of Packer at the Lake City trial under Judge Gerry. One is the mythical sentence as told by one James (Larry) Dolan, a saloon keeper and an Irishman of somewhat profane and vulgar wit. He had been a witness against Packer, having met him and associated with him at Saguache when Packer was making his getaway in 1874. It was said that Dolan had a grudge against Packer and had threatened to kill him if he were acquitted of murder. He maintained a keen interest in the case and was the first man uptown after the trial. His story goes thus:

"Well, boys, it's all over, Packer's t'hang." Pressed for particulars, Larry took an important pose before the saloon crowd and in a leering tone delivered what he claimed was the sentence: "The judge says, says he, 'Stand up, y'man-eatin' son of a bitch, stand up!' Then pointing his trembling finger at Packer, so mad he was. 'They was seven dimmycrats in Hinsdale County, and ye eat five of them, God dam ye! I sentins ye t' be hanged by the neck until ye're dead, dead, Dead! as a warnin' ag'in reducing the demmycratic populashun in the state.' "

Then there is the true intimate story of the sentence that has gained notoriety throughout this continent and has been told around the world. "The pronouncement of the actual sentence by Judge M. B. Gerry is one of the most beautifully phrased and impressive documents in western criminology. Its delivery was most impressive and affecting in the extreme—to the judge, who only with great exertion controlled his emotions, to spectators and to the prisoner, who maintained his composure well under the mention of father and mother." The true sentence follows:

The Sentence

"It becomes my duty as the judge of this court to enforce the verdict of the jury rendered in your case, and to impose on you the judgment which the law fixes as the punishment of the crime you have committed. It is a solemn, painful duty to perform. I would to God that the cup might pass from me! You have had a fair and impartial trial. You have been faithfully and earnestly defended by able counsel. The presiding judge of this court, upon his oath and his conscience, has labored to be honest and impartial in the trial of your case and in all doubtful questions presented you have had the benefit of the doubt.

"A jury of twelve honest citizens of this county have sat in judgment on your case and upon their oath they have found you guilty of wilful and premeditated murder—a murder revolting in all its details. In 1874 you, in company with five companions, passed through this beautiful mountain valley where stands the town of Lake City. At that time the hand of man had not marred the beauties of nature. The picture was fresh from the hand of the Great Artist who created it. You and your companions camped at the base of a grand old mountain, in sight of the place you now stand, on the banks of a stream as pure and beautiful as ever traced by the hand of God upon the bosom of the earth. Your every surrounding was calculated to impress upon your heart and nature the omnipotence of God and the helplessness of your own feeble life. In this goodly spot you conceived your murderous designs. You and your victims had had a weary march, and when the shadows of the mountain fell upon the little party and night drew her sable curtain around you, your unsuspecting victims lay down on the ground and were soon lost in the sleep of the weary; and when thus sweetly unconscious of danger from any quarter and particularly from you, their trusted companion, you cruelly and brutally slew them all. Whether your murderous hand was guided by the misty light of the moon or the flickering blaze from the campfire, you only can tell. No eye saw the bloody deed performed; no ear save your own heard the groans of your dying victims. You then robbed the dead of the reward of honest toil which they had accumulated; at least, so say the jury.

"To the other sickening details of your crime I will not refer. Silence is kindness. I do not say these things to harrow up your soul, for I know you have drunk the cup of bitterness to its very dregs, and wherever you have gone the stings of your conscience and the goadings of remorse have been an avenging Nemesis which has followed you at every turn in life and painted afresh for your contemplation the picture of the past. I say these things to impress upon your mind the awful solemnity of your situation and the impending doom which you cannot avert. Be not deceived. God is not mocked, for whatsoever a man soweth, that shall he also reap. You, Alfred Packer, sowed the wind; you must now reap the whirlwind. Society cannot forgive you for the crime you have committed. It enforces the old Mosaic law of a life for a life, and your life must be taken as the penalty of your crime. I am but the instrument of society to impose the punishment which the law provides. While society cannot forgive, it cannot forget.

As the days come and go and the years of our pilgrimage roll by, the memory of you and your crimes will fade from the minds of men. With God it is different. He will not forget, but He will forgive. He pardoned the dying man on the cross. He is the same God today as then—a God of love and mercy, of long-suffering and kind forbearance; a God who tempers the wind to the shorn lamb, and promises rest to all the weary and heartbroken children of men; and it is to this God I commend you. Close your ears to the blandishments of hope. Listen not to its flattering promises of life; but prepare for the dread certainty of death. Prepare to meet thy God; prepare to meet the spirits of thy murdered victims; prepare to meet that aged father and mother of whom you have spoken and who still love you as their dear boy.

"For nine long years you have been a wanderer upon the face of the earth, bowed and broken in spirit; no home, no loves, no ties to bind you to earth. You have been, indeed, a poor pitiful waif of humanity. I hope and pray that in the spirit land whither you are so fast and so surely drifting, you will find that peace and rest for your weary spirit which this world cannot give.

"Alfred Packer, the judgment of this court is that you be removed from hence to the jail of Hinsdale County and there be confined until the 19th day of May, A.D., 1883, and that on said 19th day of May, 1883, you be taken thence by the sheriff of Hinsdale County, to a place of execution prepared for this purpose at some point within the corporate limits of the town of Lake City, in the said Hinsdale County, and between the hours of 10 a.m. and 3 p.m. of said day, you then and there, by said sheriff, be hung by the neck until you are dead, dead, dead, and may God have mercy upon your soul."

Packer had served only eight years when, through the efforts of a "sob sister," Polly Pry, he was out on parole. The December 15 issue of *The Denver Times* gave a review of the case and carried the headline: "An attempt to get Packer, the man-eater, out of the pen."

The case was argued before Judge Bailey of the Canon City District Court. Lawyer John R. Smith asked for release on the grounds that there was no such thing as cumulative sentence—Packer had been sentenced eight years for each of the five men murdered. Judge V. G. Holiday of Fairplay, district attorney for the Eleventh District, was called upon to represent the people.

At the first trial Packer was on the stand for six hours. He told a feasible story that he stuck to until his death. He claimed that he had wandered from the camp to try to find help and when he came back Bell had gone berserk and killed the others. Packer said Bell attacked him and that he had been forced to kill in self-defense.

Paul H. Gantt, Denver attorney, in his book *Alfred Packer, The Man Eater*, points out that Packer could have been telling the truth—that he was convicted on circumstantial evidence, as Packer never admitted killing anyone but Bell. After his parole he lived in a little shack in Littleton on a $25 a month pension. He was a Civil War veteran, as was W. I. Edgerton, who lived in Lake City in 1883 and attended the trial. By a strange coincidence, he also lived in Littleton at the time of Packer's death in 1906 and assisted at his funeral

A number of years ago an Alfred Packer Club was organized in Denver by young Republicans. Gene Fowler, author of *Timberline*, which contains the story of Packer, was one of the card holders. Copies of the cards were made later and passed out to numerous Republicans. I have one of the cards, given to me by the late Henry F. Lake, Jr., owner of the *Gunnison News Champion*, for whom I started writing in 1933.

Alfred Packer, "The Man-Eater," 1883.

Hinsdale County Court Room. Scene of the trial of Alfred Packer on charges of murder and cannibalism in 1883. Most of the Court House has been remodeled but this room remains the same.

SHERIFF CAMPBELL SHOT DEAD

This story was taken from the *Silver World* of Lake City dated April 9, 1882.

A most foul murder was committed last Wednesday morning about two o'clock, the victim being E.N. Campbell, the sheriff of Hinsdale County.

A resident on the east side of town removed from there a few days ago leaving some articles which, a day later, he noticed had been changed in position. He then suspected that a robbery had been contemplated. On the same mesa, but a few lots further north, stands a large cottage built by T. W. M. Draper, now owned by Mr. W. G. Luckett, vacant except for some carpets, a furnished bed and a few valuable articles of furniture.

When Mr. Luckett went to his house, finding some of his articles removed, he reported it to Sheriff Campbell and he, with Claire Smith, determined to watch over the house. Gaining a key from the owner, they prepared for a cold night's vigil and concealed themselves in the hall. About one o'clock a noise was heard at the kitchen door; Campbell was standing with his left side next to the door jam. Smith was kneeling beside him. Both had their guns in their hands. The door opened, and a step was heard on the threshold. The figure then struck a match; it was out in a second, but it had burned long enough for both men to see that the thieves were armed. Instantly Campbell said "throw up your hands," and fired; he was met with a simultaneous fire from the murderer's revolver; the ball was fatal and he said, "Oh, I am shot," and fell lifeless into Smith's arms. The latter eased the dying man to the floor and ran out, but could not see which way the assassin had fled. Upon getting help they discovered Campbell so covered with blood that they thought the bullet had entered his head.

It is fortunate for the ends of justice that there were two men on guard and one escaped injury and could testify as to the identity of the murderer. There were two men, but only one fired. These men were George Betts and James Browning, proprietors of San Juan Central, a dance house of the city.

As soon as the alarm was carried to the city, armed scouts were sent out on horseback, capturing both of the men, arresting them and taking them to jail. Immediately upon capturing the murderers, although at an early hour, there was talk of lynching them. Better council prevailed and they were guarded by an armed squad from the Pitkin Guard.

After post-mortem was held they learned that the ball from Betts' gun had passed through a pane of glass in the kitchen door and then directly through the side of the house.

After hearing Officer Smith's testimony, he being the sole witness, the jury returned a verdict that E.N. Campbell came to his death by a shot from a pistol in the hands of George Betts and that James W. Browning was an accomplice to the crime.

Immediately upon receiving the verdict from the jurors, the men were ordered manacled and placed in the inner cell. Here they remained until the beginning of their last journey.

Two murderers hanged "sucumdum artem," but without ceremony. All day Wednesday groups of citizens discussed the events of the early morning and when informed of the nature of Smith's testimony, that by a lighted match struck by the murderer as he entered the house, he identified George Betts and James Browning. Feeling ran high against the men. As a cyclone gathers its deadly power, so did the tempers of the people gathering together the resolution that during the night the murderers should be hurled to hell. Accordingly, a rendezvous was appointed near the house of the dead sheriff and at about 11 p.m. men were seen to go silently and quietly to a secluded place among the willows. No spectators lingered along the streets. They formed a crowd in the vicinity of the Court House, awaiting the arrival of the executioners. These were masked and armed with revolvers. Some bore the rope, properly knotted, while others covered heavy sledges with which to burst the jail doors. After the hour named the party rapidly augmented in numbers until it seemed to include every able-bodied man in town. Few and short were the words they spoke and these were imparting instructions to positions and particularly orderly and silent movements. Meantime the bright rays of the moon were shining on the east side of town and left the valley in shadow.

While waiting for the moon to be at a proper angle, three citizens tried to dissuade them from hanging Browning, as he was guilty only of burglary, but they were met with indignant words of contempt.

They formed their line of march, rifles being in front of the masked executioners followed by their calm assistants; thence to the Court House where not a word was spoken. The only sound was a small metal whistle blown as they came in sight of the guards at the jail. There was light enough for the guards to perceive the leveled rifles preceding the column and as it advanced one of them cried, "Halt." No halt occurred and a hoarse voice behind the line of guns cried, "Throw up your hands."

Other voices said, "Don't shoot and we won't." The guards stood in a row with their hands up, having done their duty to a point where human nature must give way. They were disarmed and went their way among the spectators. Instantly the stalwart bearer of the sledge struck a death knell upon the bar and lock of the outer door and the blow was followed with the discharge of pistols, all warning the inmates that their hour had come. Blows were rained upon the fastenings, consuming twenty minutes of time, yet they remained firm. One more Viking blow by a fresh man sent the bar off and a few more burst open the door.

All was clear, and at the cry, "The ropes, the ropes," a few men entered the vestibule and dragged Browning out of the cell. He was held by the manacles, but with the strength of a bull he plunged with lowered head into the midst of the flashing circle of revolvers. Five times the rope twisted over his head, but he managed to twist out of the loop begging for friendly aid and not to be hanged. At length his arms were held down and the loop placed around his neck so firmly that he could not remove it; thereafter he said nothing. He was assured there was no mercy for him, as he was considered as guilty as Betts.

Meanwhile, there was delay in getting the rope for Betts through the crowd to the watchers near the cell. It was finally fastened around his neck and as he emerged from the jail door he asked for a chew of tobacco, cursed his custodians, but was soon given to understand that friendly aid would not be forthcoming.

The leader said, "To the Ocean Wave Bridge." The crowd fell in step and moved on with the two men with ropes fastened about their necks. After several minutes of silence the murderer asked if he had a friend in the crowd and was told he had not. He then asked for a certain man, but he was not present. The crowd told him they would deliver a message to him. He then asked that the news never reach his mother or his friends as to how he met his death. "I want my body taken down to the house," meaning his dance hall. And with this he ceased talking as they were nearing the place of execution. Two brothers and brothers-in-law of Sheriff Campbell met them and spoke to the men as they passed.

The fatal bridge spanning the Lake Fork just above the Ocean Wave Smelting Works was reached and Betts was led under the east beam and the rope thrown over it. It was then observed that his knees trembled. The rope was adjusted but not tightened until they saw that Browning was ready for suspension. "Up with them" was called and they were both instantly drawn upwards about five feet and a moment later within a few inches of the beams. The ropes were made fast to the side of the bars. With the exception of three vain attempts made by Browning to seize the rope with his manacled hands, each attempt being weaker, neither struggled.

Justice being satisfied according to the light given the people in view of former laxity in punishing crime, the crowd returned to their homes. The bodies were left suspended until Thursday after the Coroner's jury, when friends cut them down and took them to Browning's home.

The bodies of Betts and Browning were buried next day, followed by numbers of habitues, both male and female, of the dance hall. Others were compelled to attend to make a decent burial among people, but the majority was not in favor of the ghastly crime the men had committed. Yet someone must offer prayer for the deceased and they placed them in their last resting as best they could.

So ends the chapter of the plainly told story and the close of the career of two young men, who no doubt had mothers who held them close to their hearts when they were little fellows, never dreaming they would meet their Master in such a way as this. But it is none the less true.

This horrible crime was committed on Wednesday, April 26. This was the date regularly celebrated by the IOOF lodge, of which Sheriff Campbell was a member. As Mrs. Campbell stood pressing her husband's suit in preparation of the event, a tear fell on the garment and she had a dread premonition of something fearful about to happen. There was no celebration, and Sheriff Campbell was buried in the suit so carefully pressed by his wife.

Funeral services were conducted at the Presbyterian Church under the auspices of IOOF Silver Star Lodge. All public buildings were draped in mourning and the flag at the Court House flew at half mast.

The house where the murder was committed was originally built by Draper, who was superintendent of the Golden Fleece. It was bought some years later by the Mining Association headed by Col. C. F. Meek, and remodeled and modernized to be used for a hospital. The first bathtub brought into the town was for this hospital and is now in the possession of the authors, and is still in use.

The old "stage stop" and road leading to it. This was used as a "stop over" by stages going over Stony Pass to Silverton and Del Norte and was kept by a man named Galloway. Pictures by Mabel Wright.

THE DUEL
As told by William P. Harbottle while working for The Silver World

I came to Lake City early in September, 1877, when it was fondly designated by the associate editor of the *Silver World* as the "Metropolis of the San Juan."

I was a stranger in a strange land, broken in health and almost broke, with but two slight acquaintances, made in Del Norte—among the energetic builders of the new town. I remember how the sounds of carpenters' saws and hammers were heard through the night.

I had come to Colorado unarmed and during my residence in Lake City I saw several incidents of misuse of guns, and have always held that disputes could be more easily and satisfactorily settled than by making a lead mine of the other fellow. This philosophic remark leads up to a very amusing incident, wherein two men, each armed with double-barreled shotguns, played one act of what was, to one, a moment of tragedy; to all others present, a roaring farce. I call my story "The Duel" and it happened thus:

In the spring of 1878, when I was doing a little work in the newspaper office, a stranger came in and told me a duel was about to come off and if I wanted an item for the *World*, to be present. My informant wus called "The Taylor" and he was the chief promoter of the affair, in that he was convinced little "Doc" Kaye had insulted him so grossly that nothing short of amends provided by the code duello would suffice to heal the hurt.

The doctor was a small man, all legs (usually encased in boots), and wore a broad-brimmed white hat.

The scene of the *affaire d'honneur* was near old Charley Allaire's cabin—the little flat then covered with snow. The challenged party chose shotguns. The valiant little doctor was in dead earnest. Seconds were chosen, the guns gravely inspected, then loaded, the contestants placed in position and the provisions of the contest and laws of the codes fully explained.

The little doctor was the only person present who was not in on the secret, which made the whole thing more farcical. He loaded himself with the kind of ammunition not purchased in hardware stores and was as bellicose and courageous as Goliath of Gath. His opponent was calm and dignified, made it seem to all present that this was the most solemn hour of his life. We who were in on the secret repressed our mirth and, as soon as positions were taken, fled to the shelter of adjacent rocks.

The count was made by Taylor and at "three" both guns awoke the echoes along the cliffs of Henson Creek. The doctor fired point blank, his opponent wild, the gun falling from his nerveless grasp as he fell flat on his face in the snow which was instantly reddened with his "life blood" — a sponge-full of red ink. The doctor stood a moment as if horror-struck, then dropped his gun and fled toward town, followed by the crowed.

Just outside the old toll gate there was an old adobe house, near the end foundation of which the rain had washed a hole. Into this the doctor plunged headlong, but could not do much more than the ostrich does when pursued — hide his head, leaving the rest of his body exposed.

Taylor extracted him and the crowd escorted him to Frank Melvin's "office," and here, to his utter astonishment and joy, the enemy, whom he had just seen fall and die in the snow, was the first to greet him and suggest a method for liquidating damages.

To this the little doctor assented — the vote by Taylor and the crowd ratifying — and, thus, happily terminated the first and only real fair and square duel ever pulled off in the "Metropolis of the San Juan."

HELL'S ACRES

Some historians refer to one section of the town of Lake City as "Hell's Acres. It was more commonly referred to as simply "The Red Light District."

This district was on the south end of Bluff Street. I can remember when it was not considered "nice" to even say "Bluff Street," although it really was the name of the street, so named because of the towering bluffs on the west.

Some of the "girls" of this district were there simply because it represented the kind of life they wanted to live. However, there were some who were forced there by circumstances. When I was a young school teacher I talked to one such girl, who had married and whose husband was on the school board where I taught. She told me that, as a young orphan, she had heard of the good times in Lake City and had come here hoping to find work, and unable to find the work she sought and without money, had fallen prey to one of the so-called "Madames," one of the owners of the "Houses." She was very much ashamed of the life she had led and as she told me her story the tears streamed down her face. She was very fond of children and I once said to her, "Edith, why don't you have a baby of your own?" Her answer was vehement—"What, and have someone tell an innocent child some day that his mother was a wanton woman?" She also told me that she was not the only girl there who had not wanted "to be bad."

There was a "girl" named Maggie Hartman who, hearing of a miner named Crowley being ill with pneumonia in his cabin near Sherman, offered to go to his cabin and care for him when it was learned that there was no way to get him to town. She stayed with Crowley a week before he could be brought to town, and due to the cold and exposure she suffered, she too, came down with the disease. Men started to take her to town on a toboggan when a storm came up and they were forced to stop at George Boyd's cabin. Mrs. Mary Franklin had the girl brought to her house later, where she died. Reverend George Darley of the Presbyterian Church was asked to preach a funeral service for her. He not only consented, but went to the "House" and shook hands with the "girls," speaking a kind word to each. Maggie was not a church member, but she had proven herself a Good Samaritan.

A sad incident in one of the houses at "Hell's Acres" was the shooting of a young man, one Louis Estep, by the girl he had hoped to marry. He had gone there to see her just as another man was forcing his attentions upon her. She drew a gun and fired, the shot missing her aim and killing Estep. She was tried and found guilty of murder. While in prison she contracted tuberculosis and after her release returned to Lake City. Before her death she requested that she have a Christian burial from a church. M. B. Milne, minister of the Baptist Church, agreed to preach the service but was stopped by one of the trustees of the church who refused to open the church doors for the funeral. Reverend Milne followed the party to another building where the services were held and went with them to the cemetery for a parting prayer. This same minister later followed the body of a baby boy who had died of smallpox to the cemetery and held services at the grave.

The church trustee who had refused entrance to the church of the body of Jessie Landers was followed up the creek as he was returning home in his buggy, and was soundly horsewhipped by two women, both of whom had once lived on "Bluff Street." They were accompanied by a number of other residents, but it was the two women who did the whipping. I, Clarence Wright, then a young boy, witnessed that whipping, and I have never forgotten it, nor the women who administered it. I was on my pony on the way to my home at White Cross when it happened.

WHEN CONGRESSMAN BELL SAT ON A STUMP AND WAITED FOR HIS LADY TO DRESS FOR THE BALL

This story was told by the late Mr. Congressman, John C. Bell. Mr. Bell came to Lake City early in 1876 when the town was a humming little log cabin hamlet. There was no railroad—all travel being by way of Del Norte over the range. Those were the days when no man locked his cabin, anybody could borrow money or buy goods on time and every man paid his debts.

"In pioneer-times," said Mr. Bell, "men lived close to nature, and were better for it. I think there were only two or three women in the town when I came, and the arrival of a strange women was a remarkable event. When a woman passed on the street scores of men would stand looking at her. All women were good looking then. We had social pleasures then as well as now, and we could get up a ball in less time than it now takes to hire a fiddler.

"One evening a party of distinguished visitors arrived on the stage and after supper a few of us decided to give a grand ball in their honor. It was decided that Mr. So and So should go after this woman and Mr. Whatshisname call for that one, and so on. I was delegated to go down in the lower end of town and bring a lady who had recently arrived in town and whose name no one knew.

"It was about 8 o'clock when I went to the cabin and knocked on the door. 'Who's there?' asked the lady, without opening the door.

"'Why we're going to have a dance tonight, and I was sent by a committee to see if you would go. My name is Bell.'

"The lady then opened the door and consented to go, but said that she would have to dress for the occasion and that as she had only one room, I would have to wait outside. So I sat down on a stump in the yard and waited. Under the most favorable circumstances a man doesn't like to wait on a woman who is fixing up for a society event, but I rather enjoyed waiting that time.

"After a while the door opened and she called to me. I thought that she was ready.

"'Mr. Bell, have you got a pin?' she called. I felt all over my clothes, but couldn't find one. I took a horseshoe nail out of my suspenders, but she couldn't use that. No other woman lived in the neighborhood, so I told her I would go to town and get a paper of pins.

"In due time we got to the ball room. There were enough women for two sets by tying a handkerchief around one man's arm. We had a good time and the *Silver World* characterized the event as the 'swellest social affair ever held in the diggins.'"

Walter Wright —playing the handmade banjo made by his great grandfather at White Cross in 1879.

W. H. BREWSTER:
THE BLACK HERMIT OF HENSON CREEK

In the early days of Hinsdale County a young colored man, W. H. Brewster, appeared one day driving a burro loaded with a prospector's outfit. Before long he made a location which he called the Morning Star. After a little work was done the showing was excellent, and white miners said "it was just a nigger's luck to find the best thing in the district."

Though the vein was never of sufficient size to enable the owner to work it at a profit, the showing continued good until an investor came along one day and offered $70,000 for the claim. Brewster looked with scorn upon the investor and held out for a million dollars. He had long had visions of going East, marrying the lady of his choice, keeping a large house, horses and servants, giving parties and dinners, and entertaining his friends in royal style. The ore streak grew smaller with the years' development, and one by one his backers grew tired of "putting up" and "pulled out."

One winter day Brewster started to go on snowshoes over the range to Silverton, where he hoped to interest someone to help him work his claim. He froze his hands and feet, and as a consequence had only a part of finger and thumb on each hand.

Since that misfortune the working of his claim became exceedingly difficult. Holding a hammer by the aid of a sling, and turning the drill with half a finger and thumb is a thing that not one man in ten thousand would attempt, but if Brewster had lost both arms he would probably have tried to mine with his feet.

For years he had been pounding away in this manner, living alone except for the company of his little dog. Then one day his cabin burned and later his dog died. He moved to another cabin and then lived entirely alone.

Wandering about in an aimless way all day with his gun on his shoulder, plodding through deep snow in winter, returning to his cabin at night, sometimes with a snowshoe rabbit or a mountain quail for his supper, and then sitting before his fire dreaming of the time when he would "strike it rich." In the summertime he would subsist on fish and berries. People wondered how he lived.

Game became scarce. A hunter might travel all day without seeing a rabbit. The old settlers along Henson Creek said that all the groundhogs had been eaten by Brewster as for some time none were seen in this vicinity.

It began to be noticed that Brewster was acting queerly. He labored under the delusion that parties were trying to rob him of his mine. One day two tramps stopped to rest by a large rock and when Brewster saw them ran for his gun. The tramps saw him return with the gun and ran themselves.

A climax was reached when one day Brewster came to town with a rope. He went to the home of Mrs. Willis Williams, a colored woman, and started to hang her, saying that he had been commanded by the Lord to hang all women this year. Mrs. Williams escaped and Brewster was taken in charge by the sheriff, W. P. Hunt, father of the author. Brewster was convicted of insanity and taken to the asylum at Pueblo. The starving and brooding that was his lot for years would have affected many another man likewise.

Pike Snowden—early-day pioneer, noted for his far-fetched tales.

TALES OF PIKE SNOWDEN

No one seems to remember just when Pike Snowden came to the County, but everyone living here before Pike died, knew about him and his wild tales. Pike was a short rather heavy-set little man with twinkling blue eyes. He could neither read nor write, but he was nobody's fool. He found him a mine, built a cabin on one of the most beautiful spots one could wish to see, and settled down to working his assessments.

His cabin was above the road that led to Capitol City, up Henson Creek. In the early days when there was a daily stage to Capitol City, Pike would be down on the road to speak to the stage driver, perhaps to send an order to town or to get what he had ordered the day before.

He always had a story to tell, no matter what subject came up. One time the conversation was about hunting and Pike came up with, "Speakin' of deer, reminds me of one time I was chasing a deer out on the plains with a bunch of dogs. That deer could shore run, but finally my dogs caught up with him and was just about to grab him, when he up and clum a tree." I said, "hold on there, Pike, you know deer can't climb trees." "But," said Pike, "this one had to."

One day Pike said he had his fortune made. He wondered why he had not thought of it before. Asked what he was talking about, he answered that he had made an invention.

"What invention?" he was asked.

"A contraption for battleships," he answered. "Instead of putting steel on battleships, I'm going to put rubber, yes sir, rubber thirteen foot thick. Bullets can't go through rubber that thick, and iffin they hit an iceberg, instead of being smashed, they'll bounce right away from it."

Another time Pike told about being on a train that was held up by bandits. He said he got away and was running down the hillside away from the train and while he was running, a jackrabbit jumped up out of a bush and ran along beside him. After stepping on the rabbit several times Pike said he yelled: "Git outen the way, and let somebody run what kin."

The Hough Fire Company gave a Masquerade Ball each year on February 22. Invitations were sent out to all eligible to attend. One year an invitation was sent to Pike. On the invitation were pictures of hook and ladder and bucket brigade. When the mailman had delivered the invitation to Pike, he delivered a thunderstorm. Pike could not read, but when he saw the pictures on the invitation he went wild.

"Tarnation," he exclaimed. "Tarnation," was all he could say. Finally, when he could talk, he said, "I got the bucket, all right, but domned if I got the ladder and them other things, 'n bedad, if I'll pay for 'em." He thought the invitation was a grocery bill.

"Pike," I said one day, "tell me about some of your experiences of the early days." Pike scratched his head and thought for a minute before answering.

Then he said, "Well I don't know what to tell you about onless I tell you about the stage I drove in the early days here."

"That will be fine," I said. "Where did you drive this stage?"

"Between here and Californie. I forget just how many horses I had, but I had so many, and the roads was so windin' that after I hitched up in the mornin', I never saw my leaders again ontil night."

When the telephone line was put up to Capitol Pike was asked if he did not want a telephone put in. "What do I want with a telephone?" he asked. "When I want to hear anything, all I got to do is hook a forked stick on the wire and put the other end in my mouth and I kin hear everything that's said."

It was as much fun to watch Pike's face when he was spinning a yarn as it was to listen to him. When he started to talk he would look straight at one for a second, blink his eyes, spit out his tobacco juice, and then start to talk. The gestures accompanying his yarns were worth seeing, and often he would pick up a stick and try to illustrate his story in the sand.

Pike's stories were often made more interesting by his dog. Spot had been with him so long folks said they looked alike. When Pike was telling a story Spot would watch his every move, and he always knew when the story included him.

"Why should I get lonesome? Ain't I got Spot?" he answered when someone asked him if he did not get tired of living alone. When asked why he never married, he answered, "Git married and have some woman kick Spot around? I should say not. Besides Spot kin do anythin' a woman kin. Ef I git

147

drunk, and don't come home, Spot comes after me and puts me to bed. And ef I don't feel like gittin up in the morning he puts the coffee on and calls me when it's done. A woman would probably want ME to build the fire."

If anyone questioned the truth of Pike's stories, he better run, for Pike would start throwing things.

I had heard one of his tales about Mexicans, and asked him one day to tell it to me. "Mexicans?" Pike asked. "Oh, yes, Mexicans. Well, sir, I was firin' on the D&RG Railroad in early days and a bunch of Mexicans stopped the train. Afore I knowed what had happened, they was climbin' all over the engine. They killed the engineer, and started for me. I didn't have anything to fight with, so I just grabbed the shovel and started hittin' 'em. Fast as they came over the cab, I hit 'em over the head and the firebox bein' open, I just throwed 'em in the fire as I killed 'em. I cleaned up about fifty Mexicans, and then I moved over to the engineer's seat and started the train. An' by dad, I got her in on time too."

Pike always claimed that the reason he had no hair on the top of his head was that he had been scalped by Indians. He said his hair would never grow there again.

Another real wild tale told by Pike was about his little burro that he used to pack his ore. He claimed that one day he had the burro packed with three hundred pounds of dynamite and that as he was going along a rock fell off the cliff and struck the dynamite. "Well sir," he said, "Do you know that whole three hunert pounds of dynamite exploded at once. The cinch on the burro busted and the saddle went right up in the air with the dynamite. Thet pore little burro was so scairt, he started runnin' and ran all the way home 'fore he stopped."

Space does not permit all the tales of Pike. Suffice to say that everyone liked the old man and grieved when he died. Henson Creek did not seem the same without looking for the dear old man and the thought of another wild tale.

LENA WRIGHT

Mrs. Lena Amelia Wright was born November 27, 1857, in Fontana, Kansas, the third child of 10 of John and Willamina Low.

On March 29, 1880, with an older brother, John, and his family, Mrs. Wright joined a caravan of covered wagons on a 41-day trip to Lake City. Arriving in a snowstorm, she daily recorded in a diary the joys and delights, the sufferings and hardships, days when water and food were scarce.

On August 24, 1881, she was introduced to Harry Edgar Wright, a contract mining operator and former school teacher who had also come to Lake City in a covered wagon from Michigan. On April 26 of the following year, they were married at Fontana on the family farm. They returned to Lake City, but Mrs. Wright journeyed to Fontana for the birth of her first child, Rene Barber Wright, who is still living in Portland, Oregon. Three more children were born in Lake City. Clarence Edgar was born November 26, 1886 and still makes his home in Lake City. Clyde Bernard Wright was born September 19, 1899, and Lorena Amelia was born October 28, 1901. The high altitude and foul air of the mines brought about a lung condition in her husband and in 1904 they moved to San Diego, seeking a more favorable climate. He died there in 1905. Mrs. Wright moved to Boulder, where her oldest son, Rene, was attending the State University. Then began the long hard years of rearing and educating her children.

In 1914 she moved to Portland where she lived until she was 94 and on April 6, 1947, she moved to Corvallis where she entered a rest home. She passed away there at the age of 101 years, 9 months and 19 days. Outside of failing eyesight, her health had been good throughout her life.

On her 100th birthday her son Clarence and his granddaughter, Mrs. Wright's oldest great-granddaughter, flew to

Portland where they joined the rest of the family and all went to Corvallis to be with her.

Surviving children are Rene, Clarence, Clyde, and Lorena (Miller), 10 grandchildren and 16 great-grandchildren.

Grandma Wright at 101 years.

Grandma Wright and her family. Left to right — Rene, Clyde, Grandma Wright, Lorens (Miller), Clarence.

Clipping in Mother Lena Wright's scrapbook—

"Up Among the Clouds" causes Topaz to burst forth in poetry.
A visit to White Cross Mountain.
Special Correspondence.
Burrows Park, Colo. Aug. 1st, 1881.
Editor *Journal*: I have delayed writing for some time, owing to a great measure of mere laziness, or for other more important reasons. But trusting that you will overlook it this time will try to be more prompt in the future.

Something in regard to the beauties of nature, as they present themselves before the eyes of the seeker in the mountains of Colorado, might be of interest to some, if not all the readers of the *Journal*.

Up Among the Clouds

I

Up among the clouds, is a song that we can sing,
Sunlight floats upon them, too, and cheeriness doth bring.
Looking up above us, or even down below,
Clouds appear in either case, floating to and fro;
Never yet has grander sight come before my eyes.
Clouds are pierced by mountains, looking toward the skies.

II

The bow of promise oft appears, with its olden cast,
Still lingers, not with us, but hastens off so fast.
Just before our cabin door, it will seem to form,
As of course it always does, just before a storm
If the sack of gold (you know) were clinging to it still,
'Twould e'en been an easy task, to've gone and got my fill.

III

Together, as we climbed the hill, and breathed the freshing air,
(Twas L.H.C. and Topaz that formed this humble pair)
We viewed the mountains far and near,
And things that seemed to us quite queer,
Bearing , as we ever do in mind,
'Twas the work of God, and not mankind.

IV

Moving onward up the hill, with slow and steady tread,
Hunger overcame us, so we sat us down and fed;
Then again resumed our climb, and just before us, facin'
Lay a lovely, that we christened "Bouquet Basin";
Still we urged our way along until we reached the summit,
Feeling proud, of course, to know that we had overcome it.

V

Here we sat us down to rest, and view the country round.
It was a sight, indeed, dear friends,—that elevated ground;
Old Uncompaghre, towards the North, 'bove 14,000 high,
Pierces Heaven's purest air, and reaches toward the sky;
So we feasted with our eyes, on these things for awhile,
"Isn't it grand," said L.H.C.; said I "Well I should smile."

VI

The cross, so perfect in its form, lay upward to our left,
With its perfection there it stood, in rocks that once were cleft.
From this same cross, the mount derives the name it bears,
And from the valley, far below, shows forth the garb it wears.
But when we look upon it, sorrow fills our hearts,
For we think of ONE who died to kindly take our parts.

VII

Upon this mountain up so high, stood a wooden stake,
With names of two fair maidens, written on its break;
Streamers to its top were hung, to float out in the air,
Of red, and white and blue, noted by this humble pair.
And just before we took our leave, our names were written too,
To sleep beneath the streamers of the red, the white, the blue.

                                           Topaz

This poem written in 1881 was found in Mother Wright's scrapbook. The young maidens referred to in the poem were Mother Lena Wright and her friend Sadie Mathews, and to Mother Wright goes the credit of being the first woman to the Cross and placing the first flag there. Some years ago before her death, there was talk of placing a marker monument on the path leading to the Cross and dedicating it to her.

Many years later we, Carolyn and Clarence Wright, spent our honeymoon in White Cross, and I, too, wrote a poem which I sent to Mother Wright. She immediately wrote to ask me if I got the idea from the above poem, of which of course I had not, as I had never seen this one. So, when we visited her later, she gave me her scrapbook containing it. Following is my poem.

White Cross

There have been songs about Colorado
About the North, South, East and West;
But never a poem's been written
About the place that I love best;
High up on White Cross Mountain
Where earth truly meets the sky,
A perfect cross made by GOD'S own hand
Is a sight that meets the eye
A cross, formed by quartz of purest white—
A symbol from above,
For on a cross our Savior died
That we might live and love;
And so, GOD placed a white cross there
Where all who would, might see:
A reminder of our SAVIOR
And remember CALVARY.

                        Carolyn Wright

This poem was published in The Yearbook of Modern Poetry in 1939.

The White Cross on White Cross Mountain.

HARRY E. WRIGHT

Harry E. Wright upon finishing school, decided to strike out for himself and in June, 1876, right after graduation, he went to Kansas, where he tried teaching school, but confided to his diary that he didn't like Kansas, couldn't drink the water, and had met few people whom he liked. In April, 1877, he decided to leave for Colorado.

The description in his diary of his first glimpse of Pike's Peak goes, "I shall never forget my first view of Pike's Peak, as seen coming from Denver. I could not realize it was a mountain, for it was covered with snow, and from a distance looked like a bank of clouds."

Stopping at La Veta, he described it as being hemmed in by mountains. He found it to be the shipping point for the San Juan, and described watching the freight pile up, most of which was marked for Lake City, and decided the Lake City was the principal town. He saw freighters driving from one span and wagon to eight span with tail wagons. Mules were used by some and oxen by others.

The party left La Veta May 17 and reached Del Norte the 19th, where they met a Mr. Ward, who was in the soda water business, and was going through to Lake City with a mule team and wagon. He agreed to let them go along for $5 each—if they would walk. On the 22nd they reached Wagon Wheel Gap, which Dad described most beautifully in his diary. They visited the hot springs and all took baths. On the 23rd they reached Mirror Lake and camped there for the night. Again, Dad's description convinced us that he should have been a writer. While they were getting breakfast they were "serenaded" by a mountain lion lured there by the meat they were cooking. Dad claimed that every hair on every head stood straight up. From there they went on past Clear Creek Falls, and a poet could not have given a more beautiful description than did Dad in his diary.

Arriving in Lake City May 30, 1877, Dad found it to be more of a place than he had expected, and again his descriptions of the newly built cabins, nestled in a little flat surrounded by mountains is worth mentioning.

On June 12, with George Kutz, Dad started for White Cross, having worked in the meantime at the Gladiator Mine. He wrote that they found two post offices—one at Argentum and one at Tellurium. Argentum had a dozen houses, two stores, and three hotels, a blacksmith shop and a saw mill midway between the two towns. Tellurium had five log cabins, all joining, kept by Frank Barnes, who had a hotel and store.

Dad Describes Burrows Park

Burrows Park proper is about two and one half miles long, and not more than a mile wide at its widest place, Argentum. Cooper Creek comes in from the north and about one fourth mile below, Silver Creek comes in from the same direction. Opposite and between the two, Grizzley Gulch opens its mouth between Argentum and Tellurium. There is no very large gulch, but just above Tellurium, Cleveland Gulch comes in from the northwest and near its mouth are some very pretty falls, the highest being about sixty feet and in full view of the road. The upper end of the road terminates in the American Basin.

South of the Park is White Cross Mountain, so called on account of two bands of quartz covering each other at right angles and forming an almost perfect cross on the nearly perpendicular surface of the butte facing the setting sun, and when viewed at that time of day, shows very plain owing to the whiteness of the quartz and the dark granite in which the veins run. The cross is about 40 x 30 ft. and 3-1/2 ft. wide. I have a piece of the quartz that came from the top of the upright vein.

On May 27, 1878, Dad with several others bought the La Belle Tunnel. On December 20 of that year he wrote, "We have a post office here now but no one gets mail but our crowd."

In April 14, 1879, Dad and some friends decided to prospect the Gunnison country. They got back to the La Belle on May 14, and after working their assessments, went to work at the Palmetto on Engineer Mountain, owned by John S. Hough. They stayed at the old shaft house two miles from Rose's Cabin. Here he spent his evenings reading "Stanley's Travels in Africa" and playing chess. It was during this time he made the banjo described elsewhere.

On October 20, 1879 he wrote about attending a dance at Capitol City, and mentioned that the Lake City band had furnished the music. In November he and Jack McDermott got a contract from John S. Hough. The superintendent was George Henson. They finished their contract the last of February and went back to the La Belle.

In August, 1880, at a party at Sherman, he met Lena Low, whom he later married on April 26, 1882.

He built a cabin, and made all of the furniture by hand, each piece lovingly described in his diary—even to the tiny crib he made when they were expecting their first baby.

In 1881 he relocated the Homestake Mine and named it the Park View. This mine, with several others he located, are still in our possession.

Dad Wright wrote many pages in his diary, describing how he spent each day, and evenings, spent alone or with friends. In it he recorded all the money he earned and all he spent. He described in detail all the furniture he had made. His description of the organization of the Pitkin Guards, their meetings, target practice and marching is very interesting. The last entry made in his diary was on May 14, 1884 while he was waiting for Mother Wright to come home with their first baby.

Reading on in Dad's diary we learn that he worked on many different mines and located a number for himself.

Dad Wright Describes Handes Peak

Chat Priddy and I went up on Handes Peak last Sunday and took our dinner along. I wish I could describe the scene as it appeared to me spread out in all its picturesque beauty, but I cannot express myself what I feel when looking at such grand scenery. There does not seem to be words fitted to express them in my limited vocabulary. It needs a poet to describe the charms that such a landscape presents to the eye. I can only say that I enjoyed it beyond my most sanguine expectations. Toward the northwest in Utah the Wasache range could be distinctly seen. It seemed to be a range with a flat top or table land on its summit and the canon where the Uncompaghre river runs can also be distinctly seen, also Mt. Sneffles and the mountains above Ouray; the Uncompaghre valley and peak, Sheep Mountain on Henson Creek, Sierra Blanca in the Sangre de Cristo range, and the Needles mountains and all the peaks of importance in the San Juan. From the peak we could look into Utah, Arizona, and Colorado. If I could have all the sights of that day transferred on canvas, what a picture it would be!

After resting we came down to Crystal Ridge and got some of the "eggs." (By eggs he meant the oval shaped rocks called geods, which when broken have beautiful crystals inside.)

The diary stated that on December 9, Dad and Howard Barrett located the extension of the Hidden Treasure, and called it "The First National." When they ran out of money they would work at some other mine. One man gave them a short check and they had to limit their "grub bill."

From Dad Wright's paper we learn that he served in many offices in the County, having served as justice of the peace, clerk and recorder, county commissioner and county judge. In 1890 he served as census taker.

By 1904 he had contracted that dread disease of miners and the family moved to San Diego, hoping that his health would be benefited. But he passed away there in 1905. His body was shipped back to his beloved Colorado for burial.

Edith Mountain and surrounding country at White Cross location of the Wright Mines.

Looking north from Edith Mountain toward Red Cloud Peak.

Crookes Falls during high water, 1928.

J. A. Woods' mule team on the high road to White Cross above Sherman 1900.

OTHER PIONEERS

George Darley, D.D.

Reverend George Darley, D.D., was the author of *Pioneering in the San Juan*. The book was written from personal reminiscences of work done by him in Southwestern Colorado during the "Great San Juan Excitement." He dedicated his book to his wife, Emma Jean Darley, who he said was the first minister's wife to cross the Sierra Madre Range of mountains in Colorado.

Dr. Darley was a master craftsman as well as a minister. He practically built with his own hands the Presbyterian Church and Parsonage.

We have in our possession a copy of his book, which was autographed for his friend and ours, John Maurer, in 1901. After Mr. Maurer's death his widow, Mrs. Lulu Maurer, sent it to us to be presented to the church, which was done May 9, 1948.

Mr. Maurer was an elder in the Presbyterian Church.

Tim Clauson

Tim Clauson came to this area in the 70's. He mined around White Cross and took up land above the lake still known as the Clauson place, now owned by Jack Porter of Texas. He was a friend of the blind poet Gurley and the oldest daughter was named for this poet and friend.

Charles Schafer

Mr. and Mrs. Charles Schafer came here from Germany and soon established themselves as valuable citizens.

Mr. Schafer established a hotel and trading post at Rose's Cabin, which is described in a newspaper article in another part of the book.

The couple had two sons, Louis, who became a mining engineer, and Rex, who took up art.

William Patterson

William (Uncle Billy) Patterson came to Lake City in the 70's. He owned one of the first hotels, the American House, which was destroyed by fire. He later had another hotel which he called The American House on Gunnison Avenue and The Pueblo House, Hotel and Bar on Silver Street. It was while running this hotel that we, as children, knew him. He was very fond of children and often invited a group coming home from Sunday School to have dinner with him at the hotel. He could be seen almost any day of the week, sitting outside the hotel with a pocket full of nickels which he would give to passing children. We all loved him.

Daniel McLeod

Daniel McLeod was an early-day hotel keeper. He operated several hotels, the last one being the last hotel called The Occidental (there were several Occidental Hotels during a period of years). After he sold the he turned to farming and owned what is now known as The Vickers Dude Ranch, owned and operated by three sons of John Vickers.

E. H. Biggers

E. H. Biggers had a hardware store in the late 70's. He did some mining and was county treasurer several terms. One of the early-day newspapers speaks of him as "a hard tax collector."

William Rowan

William Rowan came to Lake City as a mining man. He had charge of the Capitol City Mine. He was a very popular citizen and became State Representative. He built a beautiful home on Silver Street which stood until a few years ago when it was torn down. It had been damaged by fire earlier.

Thomas Ray

The Thomas Ray family came to Lake City in the 80's. They purchased lots on the north end of Bluff Street and erected a log house and a large log hot house or conservatory and were confident that they would be successful in raising cut flowers, and tropical vegetables. The undertaking was unsuccessful and years later when we bought the place, we raised chickens in the old hot house. There were four sons, Reti, Earnest, Guy, and Taylor. Reti became a mining engineer, Guy and Earnest dabbled in mining and finally drifted away. Taylor studied medicine and was last heard of as a successful doctor in California. The Rays were active in establishing a Christian Church in Lake City.

A. B. and I. R. Carey

The Carey brothers were in the saloon business here in the early days. I. R. died from smallpox early in the 90's. They were originally from Canada. A. B. Carey was joined later by a nephew, John Vickers, who afterwards had his own saloon. After prohibition Vickers bought the McLeod ranch, where he lived until his death. The ranch has been successfully run by his sons Purvis, Robert, and Joseph, who made it into a well-known Dude Ranch.

Moritz Stockder

Moritz Stockder came to Lake City about 1878. He was a mining engineer and assayer—U. S. Deputy Mineral Surveyor. He was manager of the Vermont Mines Company, manager of the Hidden Treasure and served in city and county offices. While he was manager of the Hidden Treasure, an Italian miner fell in love with Mrs. Stockder and forced his attentions on her. Stockder fired the man, H. Nickolii, who went back to the Stockder home and shot Mrs. Stockder through the window and then killed himself.

After the Second World War Stockder went back to Germany where he invested in German marks and died there broke. There was one son who, after his mother's death, was sent away to school. He visited Lake City a couple of times after he was grown.

John Gavin

John Gavin came to Lake City in the late 70's when quite a young man. He had snow-white hair and was called "Grey Eagle." Mother Wright, who knew him as a young man, said his hair had always been that white. He took up mining but never had very good luck. He lived off game and with an occasional odd job got by.

He once invited Joe Kirker, who had stopped by his cabin, to eat with him. He served a delicious dinner of "roast pork." As Joe left he said, "I'm sure glad I killed that ground hog. It came in handy." Joe lost his dinner on the trail, in spite of the fact that he had enjoyed it while eating. Many of the early miners used the ground hog, sometimes called woodchuck and marmot, as food. It is said to taste just like pork.

Charles Forberg

Charles Forberg came in 1878. He mined some but his chief interest was in his barber shop which he had until 1914 when the family moved to Illinois. He married Amelia Maurer, who had come from Vaud Canton, Switzerland, at the age of twenty-three to make her home with her brother, John Maurer, who had come earlier and had started a jewelry store.

Herman and Emma Mayer

Herman Mayer came to Lake City in 1874, and went back to Germany for awhile. He returned in 1876. In 1881 he married a Mrs. Emma McDowell, who, as a young widow, had come to Lake City with her young son to join her brother and sister, John and Lena Lowe. Two daughters were born to them: Mrs. Emma Liska, who still lives in Lake City and Mrs. Louise Heath, who spends her summers here and winters in Pueblo.

James F. Steinbeck

James F. Steinbeck came to Lake City in the early 70's. He discovered the great Bon Homme Mine which he sold to the Scantic Mining and Milling Company for a large sum. He also located a number of other properties which were sold. He served the county in several offices and was Lake City Mayor several terms. He and his wife built a beautiful home in Lake City which remained in the family until last year when it was sold to the granddaughter of the pioneer F. M. Mendenhall.

Henry Henson

Henry Henson was one of the first company to cross the Continental Divide in the early 70's and follow the river down to the forks. Henson Creek, which flows into the Lake Fork of the Gunnison river was named after him.

Richard James

Richard James, a Civil War veteran, came to Lake City in the early 80's. To him is given the credit of seeing that all the Civil War veterans dead in the Lake City cemeteries received Government headstones on their graves. We promised him that we would see that he, too, would be so honored after he helped get the headstone for my Dad, but he left town to live with a relative and passed away in another city. Mr. James held a number of offices while in Hinsdale County.

W. R. Davy

Mr. and Mrs. W. R. Davy came to Colorado in 1880, settling first in Capitol City. Mr. Davy at one time had charge of the famous Golden Fleece mine. Their only son, William Davy, became a mining engineer.

Henry Wadsworth Longfellow, Jr.

Son of the poet Henry Wadsworth Longfellow, Sr., owned and operated the Illinois Boy Mine and other properties at White Cross. He lived with the H. E. Wrights while living at White Cross. In 1941, his widow and sons Earl Allen and Wadsworth visited Lake City and were the guests of the C. E. Wrights.

George Boyd

George Boyd, a pioneer of the 70's started a tin shop and was interested in a number of mines.

L. B. Hunter

L. B. Hunter came in the late 70's, lost interest in mining and turned to farming.

Rex Schafer, son of the Charles Schafers, owners of the Rose's Cabin.

Miners' and Merchants' Bank, now occupied as the Elk Horn Hotel.

Old planing mill in Lake City built by Harry Youmans is still standing. Photo by Grant Youmans.

Old Harry Youmans' ranch. Joe Youmans' home on Cebolla.

Harry Youmans and C. P. Foster in from old planing mill.

Toll Gate built in 1874 at the mouth of Henson Creek Canon.

Mat Dwyer

Mat Dwyer settled in Capitol City in the early 70's. Three children were born there, and the only son is buried there. The family later moved to a ranch on the Lake Fork. Two daughters, Mrs. Annie Doran and Elizabeth Dwyer still live in Lake City and the youngest daughter, Mrs. Mary Osgerby, lives in Grand Junction.

E. C. Wager

E. C. Wager came in the 70's. He located a number of mines in the high country. Wager Bulch was named after him.

J. M. Allen

Mr. and Mrs. J. M. Allen came to Lake City in the early 70's and established a general store. Mrs. Allen with Mrs. Latimer had the only exclusive ladies' goods, and Mr. Allen had the only men's tailoring establishment. Ruth Allen, who later became Mrs. Henry Lake, Jr., was born in Lake City in 1878. Her husband was the principal of the school here in 1897-98. Their son, Rial Lake, is with the Western State College at Gunnison.

Harry Youmans

Harry Youmans came to the Powderhorn Valley in 1874, and a few years later settled in Lake City, where he started a sawmill, built a number of houses and took up a ranch on the Lake Fork which was known as Youmans Station during the period the train was running. He also built a large stone planing mill, which still stands. Two of the large houses he built are still in good condition. One is occupied by the widow of A. B. Carey, early-day saloon keeper. The other is a summer home of Louisiana tourists. The big two-story house he built for his family near the planing mill was torn down some years ago. After Mr. Youmans left Lake City to live in the Powderhorn Valley, he was associated with C. P. Foster, early pioneer, both in Lake City and Powderhorn.

Henry C. Repath

Henry C. Repath was an early-day miner, coming to the area about 1880. He will always be remembered as the man who gave his life trying to save two friends who were caught in a snowslide in 1880. He left a wife and two children: a son, Charles, who became a lawyer, and Helen, who married W. J. Furse, an early-day newspaperman. Mrs. Repath later married F. A. Ralph, pioneer miner and saloon keeper.

C. P. Foster

C. P. Foster, a well remembered pioneer in the early 70's, had his own slaughter house and ran a meat market. He succeeded Patz in the Patz and Richards store, later buying out Richards. He sold out the store to H. T. Hoffman, son of the pioneer doctor D. S. Hoffman. He was also a partner of Harry Youmans in several business undertakings. These two men were known for their great friendship through the years.

J. B. Micheles

J. B. Micheles, an early-day miner, was a partner of Richard James in several mines. He owned a pet elk, which he kept in a corral with a high board fence. A favorite story of the old-timers is that of the bulldogging of that elk by one Leon LeFevre. The elk got out of his corral and LeFevre, a large, husky man, bulldogged him cowboy fashion and held him until he could be tied with a rope. No less powerful man than LeFevre could have accomplished such a feat.

Preston Nutter

Preston Nutter was a well-known freighter of the early days in Lake City. He was associated with Frank Wheeler, who worked for him, and who, although he left Lake City for a few years, returned, bought a home and remained here until his death.

W. C. Blair

W. C. Blair was an early-day newspaperman and was for years owner and editor of the *Silver World*. He was prominent in politics and a "dyed in the wool" Republican. He served as lieutenant of the local militia, Company A, 2nd Infantry, of the National Guard of Colorado. He was registrar in the Land Office for some time. He served eight terms in the State Legislature, as either chief clerk or secretary, starting when the state was a mere infant. He, with Mike Walsh, was considered invaluable. The two alternated in office. He was appointed examiner in the Colorado Insurance Department by Governor Carr in 1939, was one of twelve delegates to the Republican National Convention in 1940, appointed deputy examiner in 1941, and secretary of the senate in 1943.

He was married to Anna Maurer, daughter of a pioneer jeweler.

George Gardner

George Gardner, a pioneer of the early 70's, was a stone cutter by trade, was interested in mining, and owned one of the first large dance halls where he played the bass viol in the orchestra. He owned and operated the Armitage, a paying mine of the time. He was active in the Pitkin Guards and was later appointed inspector general. He held several city and county offices. He was appointed adjutant general by Governor Thomas. The same year he married Mrs. Josephine Proper. They lived in a large white house on the corner of Silver and Fifth Streets, which was willed to the authors and where we still make our home.

Walter Kelly

Walter Kelly was another miner who made money in this area. He, with Carl and Albert Benson and John Gray took a lease on the Golden Fleece and struck a very rich pocket of ore. Kelly had come here in 1876, but did not make any money until he worked on the Fleece. The family lived at Lake Shore and their daughter Nancy, now Mrs. Nancy Burke, was born there in the cabin now owned by the H. G. Heaths. Mrs. Burke has been county treasurer for three terms.

Kelly used his money to build a home on 4th and Gunnison, but left soon afterward. The home is now owned and occupied by Mary Green and daughter.

The Benson brothers bought ranches in Gunnison County. John Gray built a home in Crookville but left a few years later. The house is now owned by summer tourists.

William Swank

The William Swank family came to Lake City in 1882 on the day of the hanging of Betts and Browning, a day which they never forgot. Mrs. Swank was a sister of the Hunt brothers, who had come before. Swank took up mining and died several years later of consumption. Their oldest son, Frank, took up the study of fish and had several fish lakes in the south end of the county where he raised and sold fish to the markets. His grandson, J. F. Swank, followed in his father's footsteps and today is making a series of lakes and plans on enlarging them and building a resort. He owns and operates the Lone Pine Motel in town.

Otto Mears

Otto Mears was called "The Pathfinder of the San Juan." Born in Kurland, Russia, of a Russian mother and an English father, he was sent to England after the death of his parents and later to a relative in New York. He later went to Nevada where he took out his naturalization papers and when the Civil War broke out joined the First Regiment of Volunteers of California in 1861.

After the war he came to Colorado, where he started building toll roads, one of which was the road from Saguache to Lake City, and from Lake City to Silverton. In 1926 a granite slab commemorating his work, was placed on a cliff at the edge of Bear Creek Falls near Ouray, which bore the inscription:

In Honor of Otto Mears
Pathfinder of the San Juan
Pioneer Road Builder, built this road in 1881
Erected by a Grateful People
1926.

Enos Hotchkiss

Enos Hotchkiss is credited with being the "Father of Lake City," having built the first log cabin here in 1874, which stood until 1880 when it was demolished by school children. He also built the Saguache, Lake City and San Juan Toll Road in 1874, which was a year earlier than that built by Otto Mears. Hotchkiss Mountain was named after him as was the little town of Hotchkiss.

John Crooke

John Crooke came to Lake City in 1877 and with his associates bought the Ute and Ulay Mines, described in another part of the book. He built the Crookes Smelter. He was married to Nellie Mendenhall, the daughter of another well-known pioneer, F. M. Mendenhall. After leaving Lake City he is credited with inventing tin foil.

John C. Bell

One of the best known and loved pioneers was John C. Bell. He came to Lake City in 1876, when the town was described as a "humming little log cabin hamlet."

He was the original owner of what is now known as the Valley View Ranch, which was so named and operated for years by the late W. O. Baker and wife, and recently sold to the R. E. Edmondsons.

Two daughters were born in Lake City, Mrs. Susan Bell Nickell and Mrs. Ethel Bell Stivers, both widowed and living in Denver. Mr. Bell served in many city and county offices while living in Lake City, the last one being that of county judge. He is the author of the book *The Pilgrim and the Pioneer*, in which he described many of his experiences as the "Pioneer." One of his experiences is related in this book.

George T. Lee

George T. Lee was an outstanding character of the early 80's. Here he saw a chance to invest some of his earlier gained wealth and built a beautiful home, a two-story brick house, just below Capitol City. The house included a large glass conservatory, where beautiful tropical plants were grown. The large yard was beautifully landscaped. Even the "Johhny" was a spacious brick building with a fancy roof. Large lamp posts stood on each side of the entrance to the grounds. Mr. Lee drove a beautiful coach with four horses and kept a number of servants. Mrs. Lee was an accomplished

The Lee Mansion, showing brick outhouse, 1953. Almost entirely demolished now. Photo by Warren Wright.

Willis Williams on Jim.

Lake City looking toward T-Mountain, showing Lake City Ball Park, Railroad, and Draper House where Sheriff Campbell was killed.

musician and took part in a number of the early-day entertainments.

Mr. Lee built a saw and planing mill and used to delivery shingles and lumber with pack jacks. He also built the Lee smelting works, the remains of which may still be seen.

The beautiful house has gradually fallen apart, but the remains of it can still be seen, and it is one of the most photographed places in the country. The beautiful stairway to the upper story was stolen many years ago and later appeared in one of the hotels.

T. K. Wonderly

T. K. Wonderly came to Lake City in 1880 to be foreman of the *Silver World*. He became a best-known authority on all branches of printing art in this section of the country. While foreman of the *Silver World* he won an award for an example of the best job printing. He was an uncle of the late Mrs. W. C. (Anna Maurer) Blair.

R. E. Penniston

R. E. Penniston came to Lake City in the early 70's with an ox team. Originally from the South, he came here from Las Animas, where he had served as postmaster. He located what is still known as the Penniston Ranch at the foot of Slumgullion. He was a friend of Otto Means and at one time took care of the Otto Mears Toll Gate. He is said to have shipped the first ore from the Independence Mine, of which he was the owner. He also worked for the Crookes Smelter. He was at one time the owner of one of the first light plants, and owned and operated three stores in Lake City. His name appears on the programs of several of the early-day entertainments. The last years of his life he spent in darkness, having become snow blind, and later totally blind. He had a sister, Catherine Elizabeth, who lived with him many years. He married the widow of another pioneer, William Swank, and they had one daughter, Ruth Penniston Vernon, who still makes her home in Lake City.

Webster Stanley Whinnery

The oldest living pioneer of the Hinsdale and Gunnison area is Webster Stanley (Webb) Whinnery.

Born in Salem, Ohio, July 3, 1865, he came west when a mere lad with his parents, John E. and Mary Faucett Whinnery. The couple settled on land in Hinsdale and Gunnison Counties, which has since been in the family. It is now farmed by the great-grandson of the original owners, Robert Whinnery.

Mr. Whinnery still claims he married the prettiest girl in the area, Miss Finella Fueller, who came here when her father served as a Presbyterian minister.

They were married at the Presbyterian Church Wednesday evening, March 27, 1895, with Rev. Charles Fueller, father of the bride, officiating.

Mr. Whinnery had had a varied career as a storekeeper, stockman and as a public servant. He served as county assessor and as county commissioner of Hinsdale County and in 1903 was elected on the Republican ticket to serve in the House of Representatives under the Peabody Administration. He was a delegate from the two smallest counties, Hinsdale and Mineral. It was during this time that this author was sent by Mr. Whinnery to take some papers to Governor Peabody, who was passing through Sapinero.

Mr. Whinnery's ability as a public speaker was readily recognized and he was soon making minority reports in the legislature.

In 1913 he met his first defeat in public office when he ran for U.S. Congress against Edward Taylor. However, undaunted, he continued keeping up with world affairs and taking an active interest in politics. He has acted as delegate to many state conventions and assemblies.

The Whinnerys had one son, who passed away some years ago when he was serving as Gunnison County assessor. Two grandchildren are living, Robert Whinnery, who operates the Whinnery Ranch on the Lake Fork, and Mrs. Betty Mull of Milwaukee, Wisconsin.

The nonagenarian was recognized at a Republican rally held in Gunnison on November 15, 1961, for his faithful service to the Republican party and to his country. About one hundred and fifty guests attended the dinner. U. S. Senator Gordon Allott from Colorado was the speaker of the evening, having chartered a plane to fly in for the occasion.

At this meeting, we, Carolyn and Clarence Wright, were called on and Clarence told of attending the wedding charivari in 1895.

Mrs. Whinnery passed away last summer (1963) as a result of a broken hip injury suffered in a fall. Mr. Whinnery, who had also fallen and broken his hip, recovered and is still living at this writing.

D. C. Baker

D. C. Baker first came to Lake City in the spring of 1875, and settled on the ranch now known as the VC Bar. In 1882, he returned to Windsor, Missouri, to marry Miss Virginia Collins, whom he brought to the pioneer home. There were seven children born there, three of whom are still living. Their oldest daughter, Mrs. Lillian Brooks, now of Chicago, wrote us that she first learned to read from the newspapers with which their first log cabin was papered. The second daughter, Mrs. Laure Nettles, lives in Chicago with her sister. The only surviving son, Alva Adams Baker, lives in Arizona.

When Mr. Baker brought his bride home, they came to Alamosa by train, then to Lake City by stage coach by way of Wagon Wheel Gap. The bride's trunk was dumped off as too heavy, and she was sure that she would never see it again, but it was brought in later, much to her delight.

Everything was freighted in with oxen and covered wagons. The road at that time ran directly back of the Baker ranch house.

The brick house still standing at the VC Bar was built in 1893 by the Hunt brothers (W. P. and J. A.). It is still in excellent condition.

In 1906 the sons Orvil and Alva bought the ranch and the older Bakers retired, later moving to California. After the death of Orvil in 1920, Alva and his wife converted the ranch into a tourist resort which they sold in 1946 to Orvil Dowzer. It has changed ownership several times and is now owned by a Texas group, headed by Clarence Jackson.

Mother Baker, as she was lovingly called by all who knew her, died in Compton, California, in 1933 and Dad Baker in 1944. There are still folks living who remember the wonderful times at the VC Bar when Dad and Mother Baker were living there.

William F. Green

William F. Green came to Lake City in 1894. He first worked as a fireman on the Lake City branch. In 1895 he became interested in mining and later with Charles Meyers of Gunnison bought a light plant, which was a steam plant. Later he acquired the dam at the falls and used water power. He was county treasurer of Hinsdale County for a number of years and favored the idea of combining Hinsdale with the counties of Mineral and Gunnison, an idea which met with disfavor by the majority of all counties concerned. He was married to Mary Donnell in 1906.

Mary Donnell Green is a true native. Her father, Joseph Donnell, came to the county in 1875, and settled in Capitol City, where Mary and her sister Alice were born. The family moved to Lake City in the 80's. Two children were born to the Greens: David, who lives in New Jersey, and Alice, who did not marry, and who takes care of her mother at their home in Lake City. Mr. Green passed away a number of years ago at the age of 84.

J. J. and J. W. Abbott

The Abbott brothers, J. J. and J. W., came to Lake City in 1875. They were civil and mining engineers of note. They surveyed and patented most of the mining claims in Hinsdale County and many in other counties of Colorado. Their work was ably done and their accuracy was never questioned. They built the Henson Creek Toll Road from Lake City to Engineer Mountain, known as the Lake City and Uncompaghre Road, without which neither the town nor county could have maintained an existence. Nearly all the roads in the county were built under their supervision.

Henry A. Avery

Henry A. Avery came to Lake City in 1877, where he opened a news and stationery store, which he conducted until 1891. In the meantime he became interested in real estate and represented several insurance companies. He was elected county judge in 1892 and again in 1895. He was at one time county clerk, also district clerk. He was married in 1884 to Mary E. Watson. There were six children, two of whom are still living, Marian (Mrs. Long) lives in Clifton, Colorado, and Helen (Mrs. Andrews) lives in Gunnison, Colorado.

B. F. Cummings, M. D.

Dr. B. F. Cummings came to Lake City in December, 1896. He served as county physician. He was a member of IOOF #27 and Neoga Tribe I.P.R.M. In 1897 he was married to Ida M. Beam, daughter of a well-known pioneer, T. M. Beam. There were four children, three of whom are living. The first son,

Franklin, died in infancy. George lives in Montrose; Mabel (Mrs. LeFevre) teaches school in Gunnison, Colorado. Mrs. Cummings lives with her. Margaret (Mrs. K. G. Brown) lives in Wyoming.

George D. Bardwell

George Bardwell, a prominent early-day lawyer, came to Lake City in 1893 and was actively identified with public life. He was active in the fraternal organizations of Woodmen of the World, and the Ancient Order of United Workmen. He was married in 1896 to Miss Hannah Cunningham, by whom he had three daughters and one son, George, Jr.

F. M. Mendenhall

F. M. Mendenhall came to Lake City in 1877 and was followed by his family in 1881. There were seven children in the family. Before coming to Lake City he was a vocal teacher and he gave lessons while living in Lake City. In 1895 he operated the stage to and from Rose's Cabin. In 1905 he and his son Charles were successors to Harry Youmans in the lumber yard and planing mill east of Fourth Street. Mr. Mendenhall was always interested in cultural pursuits and often helped to put on entertainments of that nature. His grandson and namesake is still living in Lake City. He has served as councilman, mayor, and is at present the chairman of the county commissioners.

Louis Kafka

Louis Kafka, a native of Austria, came to Lake City in 1877 where he established a business. He erected his own building, which he called the OK Store, which is still standing and used for business purposes. He carried a complete line of men's furnishings. Working for him was Billy Mundell, who did shoe repairing and who, when hobnailing miners' shoes, made the pattern of the trademark OK on the soles of the shoes. Mr. Kafka also invested some of his money in mines.

Peter Kennedy

Peter P. Kennedy came to Lake City in 1878. He was a shoemaker by trade but engaged in mining for his first two years here. In 1882 he sold his interest in a store in Kansas and three years later bought a store here in which he carried a full line of boots, shoes and clothing. In the early history of the Golden Fleece mine he was a third owner, and also owned the Governor Pitkin Mine, which sold for $135,000. Active as a Baptist, he was instrumental in the building of the Baptist Church here, two of the leaded glass windows of which are memorials to him and his wife. He also erected one of the finest residences in the town in 1881, which still stands and is owned by Mrs. Ruth Vernon. He was married in 1874 to Mildred Talliaferro McFarland and some years after her death he married Mrs. Biggers. There were no children and after his death his property went to his brother's son, Lynn Kennedy, who with his widow ran the store for a number of years.

Samuel and James Watson

The Watson brothers, Samuel and James, came to Lake City in 1877. They started a very thriving freighting business and had their part in making Lake City prosper.

Sherman Williams

Sherman Williams came to Lake City with his parents in 1875. His father was a freighter and took up a ranch on the upper Lake Fork. Sherman started carrying the mail when yet in his teens, traveling from Lake City to Mineral Point and to Del Norte, part of the time in winter on snow shoes. He was later associated with the Watson brothers, and succeeded them in business. In 1888 he married Addie Watson, daughter of Sam Watson. They were the parents of three children. Addie Williams served as mayor of Lake City, the only woman mayor ever elected. Her sister Edna Watson Ramsey taught school in Lake City for many years.

J. E. Whinnery

J. E. Whinnery took up ranching, and today his son, W. S. Whinnery, owns one of the largest ranches on the Lake Fork, which is run by his grandson Robert Whinnery.

David S. Hoffman, M. D.

Dr. D. S. Hoffman came to Lake City in 1877. He practiced medicine and surgery and later owned his own drug store. He was numbered among the influential residents of Hinsdale County. He took an active part in the upbuilding of the community. In 1882 he was elected to the legislature. He served several terms as mayor and several as president of the school board. He was registrar of the United States Land Office for five years before it was closed. He also filled the office of county treasurer one term. He was married in 1885 to Miss Ida Youmans. There were three children born to this marriage: Henry, who still lives in Lake City in the same house in which he was born; Marian, who passed away in Bremerton, Washington; and Arthur, who lives in Colorado Springs. His wife died when Arthur was quite small and he later married a Mrs. Eldridge.

William G. Luckett

William Luckett came to Lake City in 1877. He was interested in mining, but his main interest was in a furniture store which he bought from George W. Perkins. He opened a branch store in Montrose and another one in Ouray, but later concentrated all his attentions to the business in Lake City. It was his furniture that was stored in the Draper house that was robbed by Betts and Browning, who later killed Sheriff Campbell. He was a county commissioner in 1895, 1896, and 1897.

W. I. Edgerton

Washington Irving Edgerton came to Lake City in 1876 where he began prospecting and mining both here and in Animas Forks. He was afterwards employed as driver for Barlow and Sanderson, owners of the stage route from Lake City to Saguache and later became agent at Lake City for the different stage companies. In 1890 he formed a partnership with O. McCreery in the hay, grain and coal business and soon bought his partner's interest. He later disposed of this business and in 1893 purchased a book and stationery business from A. M. Wilson. He served as county treasurer for four successive terms. He was a member of the town board, the local school board and in 1898 wus elected county judge. He was a member of the John Rawlings Post No. 28, G.A.R., and a member of all degrees of the IOOF. He attended the trial of Packer, the Man Eater in Lake City, and by strange coincidence, assisted as a member of the G.A.R. at his funeral in Littleton, Colorado, where he and the family had moved in 1904. His daughter Ruth, now Mrs. C. E. Stephenson, still lives in Littleton, returning to Lake City every summer with her husband for their vacation.

John Maurer

John Maurer, a pioneer business man of Lake City, was born in Switzerland, coming to Lake City in 1877. He was for many years the leading jeweler, and carried a complete stock of jewelry of all kinds. He also engaged in mining. He was a member of the board of trade and as a member aided in getting the right of way for the railroad. He was married in 1876 to Flora Blood, by whom he had six children. He later married Miss Lulu Lawler by whom he had three children. He served six years as county commissioner, was treasurer of the school board for a number of years and town treasurer several years.

"Nigger Willis"

No disrespect is meant by the prefix to Willis's name. That is the only name we ever heard him called by, although his name was Willis Williams.

Willis was the whitest black man we have ever known. We have not been able to learn just when he first came to Lake City, but he and his wife, Emily, were here when we were children, seventy years ago.

The first thing we remember about Willis and Emily is that they had a dairy across the street from their home on North Silver Street, which is now occupied by a tourist court. They were both former slaves and Willis's back was bent and scarred from the beatings he received as such. Emily took in washing, which, of course, was done in those days on the old-fashioned washboard.

Their home was just back of the schoolhouse and we children used to love going over to see this dear old couple. After we learned to read we used to go over and read the Bible to them and they loved having us come. I remember a picture they had of Abraham Lincoln in a large gilt frame. It was their proudest possession, and Emily never tired of telling us "what a good man was Lincoln."

Willis had an old white horse called Jim, which he used to deliver milk. He could often be seen riding Jim and singing as he rode along. Sometimes he would go to sleep while riding, and when he did, Jim would always take him safely home.

The school children used to borrow Jim and the milk wagon and ride around town. On February 12 and 22, we always had a parade with as many as could crowd in the wagon heading the parade, the others riding burros or walking, and always with flags flying.

When the children who had grown up loving this dear old colored couple were in high school, Willis became ill. He lived some time unable to work, but used to sit on the back porch, where we still visited him. Our hearts were broken when he died.

The report got out that Willis and Emily used to bury their money in cans in the yard, and soon a half-Negro began courting Emily. The poor old dear hated being alone so she agreed to marry him. I shall never forget her wedding.

I had been keeping company with a young Baptist minister, and one night after prayer meeting he said to me, "I have a wedding to perform tonight and you are invited."

I had no idea where he was taking me, but as we left the church we were joined by Frank Hough, son of John S. Hough, well-known pioneer and church worker. Imagine my surprise when we headed down the street to Emily's.

Emily was really dressed for the occasion. She wore a bright-colored calico skirt and a white pullover sweater. A snow-white lace curtain was draped around her head for a veil. Soon the bridegroom, Richard Price by name, came along with a gunnysack full of beer on his back. The wedding ceremony was performed and although Price insisted that we help celebrate, we took our leave. Emily only lived a few years after her marriage and Price soon married again. If ever he found any hidden money no one ever learned of it.

John Simpson Hough

John Simpson Hough, cousin of Ulysses Simpson Grant, came to the San Juan in the early 70's. He was a member of the Colorado Constitutional Convention in 1876, a member of the Territorial Legislature and in 1880 ran for governor of Colorado on the Democratic ticket against Pitkin, being defeated by a small majority. He was the original owner of the great Palmetto group of mines, from which he made his money. In 1880 he built the Hough block, beautiful brick buildings which are still standing and in good repair, now occupied by stores. Through the years he maintained his friendship with Kit Carson, with whom he shared his house when he lived in Boggsville. He inherited Kit Carson's famous buckskin coat which we often saw him wear and which after his death was placed in the Colorado State Museum, where it may be seen today.

Lake City is indebted to John Hough for the Hough Fire Company, which was sponsored and financed by him.

He served in both county and city offices, several terms as mayor, and was county judge at the time of his death in 1919.

Both Mr. Hough and his wife Mary were loved by everyone and did much for Lake City, both financially and spiritually. Mrs. Hough taught the young ladies Sunday School class, of which I was a member. Their son Frank was also active in church work and sang in the church choir of which I also was a member.

We were pleased to find the following in the *Pueblo Star Journal* January 19, 1963.

An old store ledger, containing the first account of the firm Prowers and Hough, is now in the possession of Mrs. Frank Nelson, who is a member of the Pioneer Historical Society and is the granddaughter of John Prowers, after whom Prowers County was named, and who was a prominent cattleman and businessman. Prowers was in Bent County when John Hough and his family moved there in 1867. Hough's wife was the sister of John Prowers. It was there that the Prowers, the Kit Carsons and the Houghs became friends. Hough built a huge six-room house, installing his family in three rooms and the Kit Carson family in the other three.

Hough heard that a new fort was to be built near them and bought a large stock of merchandise and started a store at Boggsville, named after his friend Thomas C. Boggs. Later he and Prowers formed a partnership and started another store at Trinidad. This partnership lasted until the death of Prowers. One of their best customers was the famous Richard Wooten, known to history as Dick Wooten.

The ledger spoken of had remained in the store until 1907 when the building was torn down, and lay with the trash exposed to the weather, where it was later recovered by Edwin Smith and was preserved by his daughter, Mrs. Nellie Grantham, who later gave it to Mrs. Nelson, granddaughter of John Prowers.

Mr. and Mrs. Thomas Beam
Jesse Beam

Mr. and Mrs. Thomas Beam and his brother, Jesse Beam, came to Lake City in 1875. Mrs. Beam was one of four women to come at this time. When we were children, Mrs. Beam used to tell us about the good times they had, even though there were few conveniences here at that time. She and the other three women were very popular at the dances and other social functions.

Mr. Beam was of an inventive turn of mind and he, with the help of his brother, invented a process for the treating of gold and silver. *The Denver Republican* of October 7, 1897, had this to say: "The Beam Process is no longer an experiment but an accepted and demonstrated success." The company was incorporated under the name of "The Gunnison County Beam Furnace Mining and Milling Company." However, it did not really prove successful.

Thomas Beam and his brother Jesse located the famous Golden Wonder, which they sold for $60,000. They also made several other sales of mining property.

Of the six children born there are three still living: L. T., a son, lives in Cortez; Mrs. Maude Cummings, widow of Dr. B. F. Cummings; and Mrs. Edna Hoffman, who married the son of pioneer doctor David Hoffman. The Hoffmans still live in the house in which he was born.

Robert Wagner

Robert Wagner came in 1875. He claimed to be the first to bring a wagon and mules over the road. They had to cut timber, to lay across gulches beyond where the toll road had gone. On the way they were robbed by the Indians who took their flour, mixed it with water and drank it. Their first gold "find" was at Larson Creek, three miles north of Lake City. Here they built a cabin which is still standing and is used by hunters during the open season.

Ida Carruthers

Mrs. Carruthers was a true pioneer woman, who came here from Georgetown and started a store for ladies' furnishings and notions. She later married E. W. Soderholm and they enlarged the store, putting in all sorts of merchandise. They purchased the large house built earlier by Judge John C. Bell and after closing their store retired to spend the rest of their lives there.

Thomas Kirker

Thomas Kirker and family came to Lake City in 1878, the following year after their son Joe and a friend Thomas Higgins had made the trip in, staked some claims and sent for the family. They came from Ohio by train to Ft. Garland and from there by covered wagons. Sons Joe and Coleman stayed with mining. Joe later became county clerk. Tom took up newspaper work and the two girls, Mary and Jessie, taught school. Mary married a pioneer freighter, George Mott, and Jessie married E. L. Sleeper and after his death Charles Sweet, pioneer store keeper.

William F. E. Gurley

William F. E. Gurley, Colorado pioneer of note and from 1900 associate curator of the University of Chicago's paleontological collection, the largest and finest of any educational institution in the world, came to Colorado in 1876, first to Denver and on to Lake City. There he located several mining claims which he worked with a pick and shovel.

In the campaign of 1876 he staged a joint debate with Senator Thomas M. Patterson in a rude log cabin in Lake City with a huge bonfire outside to keep the large overflow crowd from freezing. He was on the election board when Colorado became the Centennial State and often wrote articles for the *Silver World*.

He was a prolific writer largely on scientific and historical subjects, often turning to poetic meter in expressing the finer sentiments. His verses have been widely circulated.

Among some of the notable men with whom Mr. Gurley was associated in the early days here were H. A. Tabor, Abe Roberts, Alva Adams, Enos Hotchkiss, and James and John Comstock, who discovered the Comstock Lode. He was also a friend of Captain Henson, for whom Henson Creek was named. Tim Clawson, his oldest friend and partner, and who aided much in the history of this area, named his first daughter Gurley.

In 1893, while he was state geologist for Illinois, he learned that it was only a matter of time until he would be totally blind.

He kept on with his writing after his blindness, and each Christmas sent his friends Christmas cards with his own verses on them. For years he was known as "the blind poet of Chicago."

Mr. Gurley was married twice. His first wife died in 1918. In 1921 he married Katherine Beard, whose understanding and encouragement meant much to him in his years of dependency.

Mr. Gurley visisted Lake City in 1940, at which time he and Mrs. Gurley visited with friends and with sons and daughters of friends who had passed on. His visit to our home will be long remembered. When he learned of my desire to write, he was delighted and upon his return to Chicago sent me a beautifully bound book, *A Literary History of America* by Barrett Wendell, professor of English at Harvard.

At the age of ninety Mr. Gurley crossed the threshold into life everlasting. His friends in writing his memorial used the verse he had composed for a friend:

> Another friend has cast aside
> His earthly dust
> Another soul will now abide
> With Him we trust.
> Another spirit is enshrined
> In realms above
> Another memory is entwined
> With all we love.

The Hunt Brothers

W. P. and J. A. Hunt came to Lake City in the late 70's. J. A. remained but W. P. moved to Grand Junction, where he lived several years before returning to Lake City to make a permanent home. The brothers were brick masons by trade, and much of their work is still standing. In 1880 they built the brick house, still in use at the VC Bar, and the two-story brick schoolhouse. The schoolhouse was remodeled in 1950 and is still used. A number of other brick buildings, some still standing and some that have been torn down, and most of the brick chimneys on log and frame buildings, were built by them. William Hunt also helped to build the famous Beaumont Hotel in Ouray. They owned and sold the Pelican Mine and other claims.

About 1898 the brothers had their own brickyard and kiln in the yard adjoining the J. A. Hunt home. J. A.'s oldest daughter, Pearl McCloughan, still owns the old home and lives there part of the time. The next older daughter lives in Long Beach, California, and the youngest, Opal Lofquist, lives in

Kirkwood, Missouri. Two sons and a daughter died a number of years ago. I, Carolyn Hunt Wright, am the only living child of W. P. Hunt. The brothers were both Civil War veterans.

Andrew MacLauchlin

Andrew MacLauchlin, Sr. and family came to Lake City in 1878, having come to America from Scotland in 1852. He built one of the first log houses in Lake City. It is still in good condition and occupied by his granddaughter and husband, Mr. and Mrs. James Wells. Several of the papers of the early days speak very highly of him. He was county surveyor in 1885. Mrs. Wells is the present county superintendent of schools.

Mrs. H. E. Wright and Mrs. Moritz Stockder. Mrs. Stockder was murdered by an Italian miner who fell in love with her and was fired by her husband.

QUOTES FROM OLD NEWSPAPERS

"Enos Hotchkiss is credited with being the father of Lake City, he having built the first cabin in 1874, which stood until 1880, when it was demolished by school children."
Lake City Mining Register-January 1, 1881

"Unlike most frontier towns, Lake City attracted a superior type of newcomer."
Silver World-June 25, 1877

"The status of Lake City is far above the average of Western and Frontier cities, and no mining camp in the world can boast of more intelligent, cultured, peaceful citizenship. A street brawl is of the rarest occurrence and for months the log cabin that serves as a calaboose is tenantless."
Lake City Mining Register-1881

"The miners, not only of Lake City, but the entire San Juan area, are as a rule intelligent, sober, industrious and ambitious. There is too much activity here for drones and the 'loafer' is not known. Nearly every miner has a prospect or two of his own into which he puts his earnings."
Mining Register-1881

"Charles Schafer, one of San Juan's most valuable pioneers..."

"Judge Wright, our handsome Harry, who carries the steelyards of justice in this precinct, gave the boys a dinner Sunday afternoon in honor of his birthday. The menu was *way up*, including a superb, gorgeous, towering snow-white crusted cake, built for the occasion by one of Lake's fair damsels, and judging from the specimen, she is an expert."
Silver World

From the *Denver Post* Special, November, 1960:

"George Edwards, who was forced to resign under fire in February as county commissioner and was defeated in a bid for re-election in the primary, lost again Tuesday when two of his supported candidates, Elmer McDonald for sheriff and R. E. Gibson for commissioner, were both defeated. Two hundred thirty-five of the county's two hundred eighty-two registered voters in Hinsdale County cast their ballots. Gibson had been appointed to replace Edwards after his resignation but was defeated for re-election.

"Hinsdale County has forty-six more registered voters than the census shows residents. The county clerk says this is due to the fluctuating population. When the census was taken in 1960 the population was placed at two hundred eighteen. The registration books that year showed two hundred sixty four voters. This is due to the fact that lots of people who come here and establish residence do not remain all year round and were away when the census was taken."

"Harry Wright and wife have gone to Burrows Park for the season. We will miss them in our social circles. Hope Harry will hit it rich. No boy on top of this earth is more deserving."
Silver World

Another Pearl

"St. Peter's winged messenger swooped down on Fontana, Kansas, the night of December 9, opened the lattice of a certain dwelling, dropped a pearl and soared away. Later a message reached Harry Wright, one of our county commissioners, that he had laid claim to the gem and that in the near future it would call him Papa. Blessings on the baby boy and his mother. Dad can look out for himself. We hope that this heir-loom will grow into a Wright-eous and noble manhood."
Silver World

(The "pearl" was the oldest son of Harry Wright, Rene B. Wright, who is still living and makes his home in Portland, Oregon, where he and his wife recently celebrated their Golden Wedding.)

From the *Lake City Times* -March 30, 1893:

"A. C. Surtees and family moved down from the Ulay this week." (Surtees is the man who killed and was killed by, John Addington in a shooting scrape in 1901.)

"Larry Dolan says there are a whole lot of good men died during the past year, and he doesn't feel too well himself." (Dolan is the author of the ridiculous sentence he claimed that Judge Gerry made at the Packer trial.)

From the *Lake City Mining Register* -January 1, 1881.

"From Lake City the Rock Mountain Stage and Express Company run coaches daily to Capitol City, and Rose's Cabin, up Henson Creek Canon, and over Engineer Mountain to Mineral Point and Animas Forks, where connections are made with coaches for Silverton, Eureka, Howardsville and other points; and to Sherman, Burrows Park and up the Lake Fork of the Gunnison.

Rose's Cabin

"At the headwaters of Henson Creek and under the shadow of Engineer Mountain, at an altitude of 11,200 feet, lies the important little camp of Rose's Cabin. The camp derives its name from Corydon Rose, one of the early pioneers of the San Juan, who built the first cabins at this point in 1877. Until a year ago (1880) it was the only place of entertainment this side of the range, until Lake City was reached. The camp is surrounded by a hundred magnificant leads, the most noted being the Palmetto and Ohio Consolidated Mining Company's property. Of the latter the Dolly Varden has received the most attention and this year a lot of machinery for working the mine has been placed in position. Charley Schafer, one of San Juan's most valuable pioneers, has the principal depot for the shipment of supplies and conducts a hotel, which is a famous resort."

Note: These buildings were an enlargement of the original Rose's Cabin. Mr. Schafer constructed two large barns, parts of which are still standing and are all that remains of the once prosperous camp. In 1920 the Golconda Mining Company remodeled the barns, added a huge fireplace to the old building and also installed modern plumbing. In the late 50's the main building was torn down and hauled to Lake City where it was used to remodel the old Abbott house which had been bought by H. L. Townsend. The remains of the fireplace are still standing.

From the *Silver World* -1882:

"O. D. Loutzenhiser (Old Lot), who had sold his mine for $40,000 and gone into the stock business in the Uncompaghre Valley, sold his range interests for $90,000."

"Hinsdale County went Republican as usual. James Galloway was elected state senator; D. S. Hoffman, representative; Claire Smith, sheriff; and H. E. Wright and X. R. Callaway (Democrat), commissioners."

"Burrows Park Post Office has been changed to White Cross."

From the *Silver World* -June 25, 1887:
Walter Mendenhall, editor.

"Carl Patz and Lis Swisher are the champion pole twisters of this section."

"A whirlwind of almost cyclonic dimensions shook things up pretty lively in vicinity of the Opera House Wednesday."

The following article appeared in the *Denver Rocky Mountain Herald* dated August 5, 1876:

Lake City

"Next to Del Norte, the above town is the greatest 'commercial centre' of the San Juan mining country. Its *Silver World* gives the business census of Lake City as follows: Stores, general merchandise, clothing, grocery, 14; hotels, 3; restaurants, 3; bakeries, 4; banks, 2; millinery and dressmaking establishments, 2; boot and shoe stores, 3; jewelry store, 1; assay offices, 4; barber shops, 2; blacksmith shops, 4; tobacco store, 1; saloons, 9; brewery, 1.
In the professions there are ten lawyers and five physicians. Within a mile of town are the reduction works of the Crooke Brothers, and there are three sawmills kept busy running to supply the town with lumber. A church (Presbyterian) and a

Good Templars Lodge have been organized and a well attended school is in session. There are several other business enterprises on foot, including additional stores and reduction works. Two brickyards will soon be able to supply the building material of that kind. Buildings are springing up on every hand, in such an extent in fact, as to require close attention to keep pace with the various improvements. There are already completed, or in the process of erection, nearly 300 houses. This is not a bad showing for a town not eighteen months old.

ABOUT THE AUTHORS

Clarence Wright was born in Lake City in 1886. He attended the Lake City schools through the tenth grade, when his parents moved to San Diego, California, where he graduated from high school. After his father's death, the family returned to Colorado and settled in Boulder, where his elder brother was a senior at the State University and where he entered preparatory school. He returned to Lake City each summer to keep up the assessment on the mines. In the spring of 1908 he came back to stay. He was married to Carolyn Hunt February 25, 1911. In 1914 he was appointed postmaster at Lake City, a position he held until 1935. He and Mrs. Wright later owned and operated a cafe. In 1935 he was appointed Hinsdale County welfare director, which position he still holds, and has received a number of awards from the Welfare Department.

While he was postmaster he was awarded a silver loving cup for Hinsdale County.

Carolyn Hunt Wright was born in Grand Junction August 8, 1890. She moved with her parents to Lake City at the age of seven. A graduate of the Lake City High School, she later attended normal school at Greeley. After teaching several years, she returned to school at Western State College. She taught school both in Hinsdale and Gunnison Counties, and served as county superintendent of schools for sixteen years, her last term being from 1948 through 1958. She has worked as a newspaper reporter since 1933, writing for the *Gunnison News Champion*, *Grand Junction Sentinel* and the *Lake City Tribune*, of which she was the associate editor. She also did spot news for the *Denver Post*. She has had a number of songs and poems published. She published a short history of Hinsdale County in 1960. She has served as Cancer Captain, is chairman of the T.B. Society. She received an award for war work during the First World War, is a Presbyterian, a member of the Ladies Aid, and the Federated Women's Club, for which she was State Chairman of Conservation for four years.

ACKNOWLEDGMENTS

To our dear parents, who were thoughtful enough to keep a record of the happenings of the early days in Lake City.

To J. F. Steinbeck, early-day postmaster.

To Edna Hoffman for the use of a club paper.

To Edna Ramsey for the use of a paper written about her father's experiences.

To Grant and Margaret Youmans who loaned us pictures and talked with us about the experiences about their pioneer parents.

To Mr. and Mrs. W. F. E. Gurley for their love, encouragement and faith.

To Gurley Clawson Carr for the talks with her regarding the early days of her father, Tim Clawson, early pioneer.

To Ruth Stephenson for sharing her father's memories and loaning us one of his books.

To the daughters of J. C. Bell for their letters.

To Lulu Maurer for her letters of information.

To Ellen Wells, daughter and granddaughter of the early pioneers.

To A. P. Griffiths, son of pioneers for his interviews.

To Henry Carman who helped us to remember names and dates.

To the Hinsdale County officers: Nancy Burke, county treasurer; Jean Vickers, county clerk; and Annie Doran, county assessor.

To Henry F. Lake, Jr. former editor of the *Gunnison News Champion*, for his encouragement and help while writing for his paper.

To the employes of the State Historical Society for their patience and kindness in helping us with our research.

To Louise Heath and Emma Liska, daughters of Herman and Emma Mayer.

To Elizabeth Dwyer, daughter of Mr. and Mrs. Mat Dwyer, early pioneers.

To Lillian Baker Brooks, oldest daughter of the D. C. Bakers.

BIBLIOGRAPHY

Ordinances of Lake City, Colorado—Phonograph Printers, 1908

Pioneering in the San Juan, by George M. Darley.

Fosset's *Colorado*

Club Paper—"Lake City," by Edna Ramsey, daughter of Sam Watson

Club Paper—by Edna Hoffman, daughter of Thomas Beam

Resources and Mining Wealth of Hinsdale County, by L. A. Vinton

Memorial to W. F. E. Gurley, by the Masonic Lodge

Presbyterian Church Records

Baptist Church Records

Copies of *Silver World* from the first issue, June 19, 1875.

Gunnison News Champion

Lake City Mining Register

Lake City Phonograph

Lake City Times

Rocky Mountain News

San Juan Crescent

San Cristobal Magazine

Diaries of H. E. Wright, Lena Lowe Wright, W. P. Hunt, Lucy Hull Hunt.

Interviews: Our parents, J. F. Steinbeck, Moritz Stockder, Mrs. E. M. Mayer, Mr. and Mrs. W. F. E. Gurley, Gurley Clawson Carr, Ruth Stephenson, daughter of W. I. Edgerton, and niece of P. P. Kennedy, Mr. Prowers (brother-in-law of J. S. Hough), M. E. Childs (1906)

Letters from the daughters of J. C. Bell.

Brochures from the Chamber of Commerce of years ago when C. E. Wright was secretary

Booster Club Programs, Literary Club Programs and Church Programs

Calship Log-paper published at the shipyards at Wilmington, California.

Letters from Mary Kirker Mott and letters from Lillian Baker Brooks, oldest daughter of the D. C. Bakers

www.ingramcontent.com/pod-product-compliance
Lightning Source LLC
Chambersburg PA
CBHW070536170426
43200CB00011B/2437